D1150700

Forgiveness and Violets

ISBN: 978-1-9163262-0-0

First published 2019

Copyright © 2019 Eva Caletkova

All rights reserved. Apart from any permitted use under UK copyright law, no part of this publication may be reproduced or transmitted in any form or by any means, electronic or mechanical, including photocopying, recording, or any information, storage or retrieval system, without permission in writing from the publisher or under licence from the Copyright Licensing Agency Limited. Further details of such licenses (for reprographic reproduction) may be obtained from the Copyright Licensing Agency Ltd, Saffron House, 6-10 Kirby Street, London EC1N 8TS.

Any views expressed within this book are the sole responsibility of the author and do not reflect the opinions of any other person, publisher, company or organisation.

"Forgiveness is the fragrance that the violet sheds on the heel that has crushed it."– Mark Twain

Contents

Dreaming of Blue Jeans

When I was a child, I dreamed of owning a pair of blue jeans. It may sound ridiculous today, considering how easy they are to find, but it hasn't always been that simple.

In Czechoslovakia, blue jeans were named "rifle", after the Italian brand that contributed to the growth and success of the jean culture in Europe. When I was ten years old, the clothing stores were half-empty, and I quietly envied the few classmates of mine who had blue jeans. During communism, it was customary to pass clothes down from older to younger siblings or other family members. So, I often wore clothes which were passed on by my older cousins. Unfortunately, those bags of hand-me-downs never once contained those much desired jeans.

My father was an autodidact. He taught himself about gardening, about machines such as cars and tractors, sewing, and other matters. He was always looking for efficient solutions to his – our – needs. We needed a garden, so he studied books and magazines to find out how to take care of grass and flowers. He even created an irrigation system within the garden, so that he didn't have to water manually.

Despite facing poverty, our father wanted me and my sister to have nice clothes. So, he bought a sewing machine, and learned how to use it. Over the years, our father sewed skirts, trousers, and winter overalls called *oteplovačky*. *Oteplovačky* were warm-up suits that were very handy when practising winter sports like skiing or, in our case, sledging. He also made us simple fabric bags, that we used in primary school to carry sportswear. At that time, we were not allowed to wear regular street shoes in the classroom, so we had to carry around a second pair of shoes. The fabric bags were extremely handy in this respect.

While my father made sure that we were always wearing clean, good-quality clothes, he couldn't have cared less about modern garments. In his opinion, fashion wasn't important, and could even have a negative influence on one's personality. I begged to differ. Jeans were a symbol of freedom, fashion, and expression. As a child, my looks gave me a complex.

I was a chubby kid, dressed in modest clothes, and as such I was unpopular at school. Some pupils laughed at me and made fun of my appearance. Nevertheless, I still admired my father. He never tried to impress people; intellect and knowledge were always more important to him than material goods. There was one time, in a shoe store, where he tried on a pair of comfortable sandals, and without considering the changeable fashion, he immediately bought two pairs. He was a practical man, and preferred logic to emotion.

Most of the people who had jeans, bought them in a shop called "Tuzex". In the olden days of Czechoslovakia, Tuzex was a chain of stores where one could purchase goods from abroad. This was done by paying with foreign currencies, or with bony, which were special vouchers. Those who had no access to foreign currencies could also buy bony vouchers through the black market. The government aimed to use Tuzex as a way of taking foreign currencies from its citizens.

In Bratislava, I was once in a Tuzex store, and couldn't hide my surprise. I was shocked by what one could buy there – such fashionable, good-quality clothes, that you couldn't find elsewhere. In ordinary stores, we could only buy shirts made from low-quality, polyester fabrics that were extremely itchy and sweaty. I felt that Tuzex was an elite shop, spoiling the chosen few that could afford it. It was a shop for those who had the best connections, regime sympathisers, and the people who received foreign currency from working abroad. In short, it wasn't for people like me.

My dream only came true, after my auntie gave me a pair of her old jeans, which no longer fitted her. They were huge, so I had to use a belt in order to get them to stay around my waist. At the time, I was thirteen years old, and didn't care enough to ask her where she had found them – I was just so excited to finally have my own pair.

Today I am the proud owner of four pairs of jeans. My life changed – so did my dreams.

Apaches in a Two-Bedroom Flat

When I was little, we lived in a small, two-bedroom flat. I believe a rented home can be considered a fairly comfortable start for a family with two young children. Life was humble, but still cosy. When visiting my friends, I noticed that there were occasionally three generations living together in one flat. This showed me that there were other people who lived more modestly than us.

My first memories are from when I was four years old. I remember my little wicker chair, which I loved to sit in. I knew exactly where in the living room my chair would be, and I defended it from my sister, or any other children that wanted to sit on it without permission. To this day, I still remember the exact distribution of the rooms within the flat, and I also remember the many in-flat adventures involving me and my sister. Our kitchen was so small that it could be filled by a single kitchen unit. There was no room for a table. Standing in that kitchen, we were so cramped that we could see the spots on each other's faces.

The living room, on the other hand, was luminous and relatively spacious. When entering, one could see the children's nook on the left, with room for a small, low table and two wicker chairs. My sister and I would spend many hours playing in the living room while our mother was cooking and watching over us from the kitchen. Sometimes we managed to circumvent her surveillance. There was one afternoon, when our mother was busy cooking dinner, that we decided to improve the decor. We created a large, abstract piece of art on the wall, using pencils and felt-tip pens. The artwork consisted of letters, lines, and shapes. Much to our surprise, our parents weren't too happy with our choice in decoration!

The layout of our home was quite simple. When you entered the flat, there was a small foyer. After mandatorily taking off one's shoes, you could go left into the kitchen, or straight ahead into the living room. On the right there was a small corridor leading to three rooms – the toilet, the bathroom, and the bedroom. The bathroom served the purpose of basic personal hygiene, but it was also the place where we would wash ourselves after returning from our outdoor adventures.

As children, our fantasies were stimulated by films like *The Treasure of Silver Lake* and *Old Shatterhand*. American Western films were very popular in Czechoslovakia. Even more popular were Karl May's books, which could be found in most homes. On one occasion, my sister and I played a game called "We are Apache Indians". In this game, we pretended to be American Indians, stripping off our clothes and decorating ourselves with cosmetics. Of course, the only place we could find these cosmetics was in my mother's makeup bag — so the game only started at the precise moment when she wasn't watching over us. We started with our faces, and then extended the painting to the rest of our bodies, using lipstick, pencils, and eyeshadows. The end result was amazing, and we were proud to be members of the Apache Indian tribe! Needless to say, when our mother eventually found us, joyous and naked and covered in her lipstick, she was less amused than we were.

Looking back, I see how modestly we lived. I enjoy remembering innocent and positive moments from my early childhood. There is something special about children, who are free to let their imagination run wild.

The First Kiss

'Don't run. I will catch you anyway!
Emil, where did you hide?'

When I was a child, our playgrounds were very simply equipped, and in some cases we had to improvise. Children enjoyed a couple of climbing bars, and an area dedicated to ball games, but there was little else to speak of.

My childhood memories feel fairly fragmented. I remember many situations and activities – some of them quite detailed, others blurred. However, one thing that I remember in really clear detail, was the rope swing in our playground. This was a column that had been vertically inserted into the ground, and had two ropes fixed on top of it. The ropes were hanging half a meter from the ground, and had a knot at the far end, with a small wooden stick inserted into said knot. Children sat on the knot and, with the help of other children or by themselves, tried to either swing or spin around it. Every time two children used the ropes they would cheerfully bump into each other, again and again.

Since there were statues in both the playground and the surrounding public area, it was natural for kids to run around them. One could also find rows of vibrant concrete rings, painted in bright colours, placed next to each other. These rings formed a tunnel, through which children could crawl. While the original purpose of the rings was to support an excavation project, they became one of the primary attractions in our playground. My sister and I, along with other children, used to love playing together inside and around the rings.

When I was five years old, I fell in love for the first time. His name was Emil. I first met Emil in kindergarten, and instantly had butterflies in my stomach. Unfortunately, my love was unreciprocated. Emil was unaware of his handsomeness, but well aware of my affection for him – and therefore he ran away every time he saw me. Since he was very energetic, I had no chance of catching him.

Despite the initial rejection, I tried my luck on various occasions. Emil often played in the same playground as me and my sister. One afternoon, I decided it was time for Emil and I to enjoy our first kiss. In my mind, being kissed by surprise would be the best thing that could have happened to Emil. So, after noticing him sitting alone inside one of the concrete rings, I made my move. Partially hidden behind the entrance, I jumped out, leaned forward, and gave Emil a quick peck on the cheek. I remember being surprised by his reaction. Instead of running away, or even kissing me back, Emil started to blush. Then he just sat there, without saying a word.

I will never forget my first kiss, and neither will Emil. A first kiss is going to happen at some time in nearly every person's life. And I do believe that kissing has importance and value, rather than being just fun.

On Pigeons and Death

'Please do not kill the pigeon, please!' Nobody heard my silent screams.

My racing heart was jumping out of my chest.

Sadists! Yet another stone. Yet another smirk.

They didn't see me, but I was standing there, with no idea what to do.

Panic and horror in my little heart.

They had no mercy. It was a pigeon with an injured wing.

Unable to fly, it had become the object of their perverse game.

They threw another stone as the pigeon desperately tried to escape.

It had no chance against three cruel teens.

They threw more stones.

The pigeon was dying. I was sobbing.

They looked at me and turned away.

Once the horrible deed was done, they left, amused and satisfied.

Proudly saying: 'We finished him off.'

I was left there, standing alone, just me and the dead pigeon. Eventually, my sister approached. She took a plastic bag, and carefully scooped up the mass of feathers and flesh, before muttering something about burying the bird. Still, I stood there, with my eyes full of tears.

There are some experiences that stay with us for the rest of our lives. To this day, I still feel stressed just being close to a pigeon. I cannot bear to remember the horror that I experienced that day, and prefer to be in places with no pigeons at all. Acknowledging this feels quite strange to me. After all, surely I should have a phobia towards evil people, not pigeons?

In the past, I often remained speechless in the face of cruelty. Today I am a different person. I don't watch injustice in silence. I act. I am a volunteer and the project coordinator of a charity. I help homeless and marginalised people, by organising clothes collections and cooking in a day centre. I even promote mental health awareness, by providing information on depression.

The once silent observer has become a woman of action. I hope that my sense of justice will continue to prevail over my fears.

Cars, Vacuum Cleaners, and Other
Means of Transportation

Nowadays, when I mention the "Trabant", many people have little to no idea of what this means. However, there are some people who remember, and the thought brings a little smile to their face. For those who don't know: the Trabant was a communist-era vehicle, affectionately named "Trabi" by the Germans.

The Trabi was a small, slow, and not very attractive car. It was an everyday vehicle, not only seen on the streets of the GDR, but also in Czechoslovakia. The communist regime and the GDR supported mutual trade, and we were therefore able to buy Trabants as well. The purchasing process was complicated, as only a limited number of cars were imported, resulting in long waiting lists. In Zwickau, where the Trabant was built, it was produced in two styles: Limousine and Universal (Combi). I'm still amazed by the proud names they gave those cars. Limousine refers to something luxurious, but the Trabant was a low-quality vehicle made of cheap materials. The people buying it paid more for plastic, and less for steel. At home, all our Trabants were Combi. At first we had a blue Trabant, but later on we got a greyish-white one. My father even bought a third, damaged one, which basically served as a source for spare components.

To be honest, I didn't like our car. It was uncomfortable to sit in. Moreover, since the Trabant was a two-door vehicle, it was a pain to access the rear seats. My parents had to fold down the front seat in order for us children to enter the back of the car. Not only was the back seat uncomfortably small, but due to its engine and exhaust, the entire Trabant was a loud and environmentally unfriendly vehicle. I felt even more uncomfortable with our car after accepting a lift from fellow pupils' parents, or family friends. It was a completely different feeling to sitting in a Škoda or Lada Riva. To add to this, I was often the subject of mockery when my father parked up in front of the school. My classmates would make stupid jokes: 'Your father came to pick you up in a vacuum cleaner?' 'How many days does it take to reach home?' However, my father was just glad that his car had low fuel consumption, and that it wasn't difficult to find parking space in town.

While at the time this was a source of great embarrassment for me, looking back it is hard for me to understand my classmates' snooty comments. In truth, the cars most commonly driven at the time – such as the Wartburg – hardly stood out for their appearance or performance. There was little diversity in communism, and everything from clothes to cars looked more or less the same. I was living in a world of uniformity, and our Trabant was just one small part of this.

Waiting, Waiting, And Waiting

During communism, we had to wait for almost everything. In many cases, this was a desperate, torturous experience. When someone needed a car, they couldn't go straight to a car dealer. Cars were obtained from a state enterprise called Mototechna. Since the import of cars into the CSSR was limited, people had to wait for long periods before they received the car they wanted – which was usually just whatever they could afford. I vividly remember my classmate's auntie picking her up from school in a beautiful Ford. I could hardly resist staring, the sight was so spectacular. Or at least, I perceived it that way, because it was so unique and different from what I was used to.

Everything comes to he who waits. When it comes to patience, Slovaks say, '*Trpezlivosť ruže prináša*', which means 'Patience brings roses'. Those who wait patiently, usually get what they desire. It wasn't just cars that we had to wait for, but washing machines, furniture, and other material goods too. I still remember how happy my mother was after we finally received a new washing machine. Believe it or not, there was once even a shortage of toilet paper, so we had to cut newspapers into pieces to wipe our bottoms.

Considering the average salary, goods like furniture and domestic appliances were so expensive that one had to save money for several months in order to afford them. Another issue was the limited quantity of produced and imported goods – the lack of options in design and colour didn't make the situation any better either. The red and white of communism generally dominated the kitchens of the average household, and this included ours.

Naturally, all this waiting was no fun at all. What *was* funny were the stories written by various humorists who, after the fall of communism and with great irony, described the "phenomenon of waiting".

Various songwriters described the stupidity of the regime; Karel Kryl's songs were recognised amongst both the Czechs and Slovaks for their depth and poetic meaning. Ivo Jahelka is another singer, and lawyer, who dealt with this period in a humorous way, using socio-economic relations in his song *Balada Československá*.

It's interesting how life changes. In the past we had difficulties getting the simplest of things – things that are now all too easy to find, and all too easy to take for granted.

Exotic Fruits

When my parents started dating, my mother weighed only forty-nine kilograms. With a smile on his face, my father told her that unless she gained at least one kilo more, he wouldn't marry her. Mama (mother in the Slovak language) was not only attractive, but hardworking and determined. She left the village where she grew up and decided to study in Bratislava. The limited financial support that my grandparents could offer was not enough to pay for her studies, so she earned money by working as a clothes shop assistant.

My mother was always very active, and ambitious to learn and work. During my childhood, I often saw her reading economics-based literature and, a few years later, human resources related material. She also enjoyed reading magazines about gardening, and reading the Bible. Neither of my parents paid much attention to the newspapers – which were geared towards glorifying the communist regime. My parents had a strong sense of justice, and therefore despised propagandistic manipulation.

During communism, it was uncommon to go to a grocery store to buy exotic fruits like oranges, tangerines, pineapples, and physalis. Sometimes certain fruits – such as lychees and pineapples – could be bought in cans, but otherwise it was rare to find these in store. Luckily, we were able to grow all kinds of fruit in our garden. The climate in Central Europe is excellent for growing fruit and vegetables, and therefore my childhood was filled with the sweet taste of cherries, plums, peaches, and apples. The fruit and vegetables we harvested ourselves, usually tasted better. This was not only because of the hard work and care invested into the task, but also because my parents were careful when using fertilisers. They preferred organic manure over artificial fertilisers, and knew exactly what was going into everything they grew.

My parents loved fruit. My mother once told me how my father visited her at her student dormitory, holding a can of pineapples. He already knew she wanted to study for an exam, but instead of waiting to meet with her on another day, he had hoped that the tropical fruit would tempt her. Well, it did. Although she insisted that she had no time for distractions, she still spent some time with him.

Exotic Fruits

In Czechoslovakia, fruit brought in from abroad was often used as an element of communist propaganda. During events that the government considered important, people were given oranges and tangerines. My parents told me that fruit was also made available during the Spartakiad, a sporting event in which people exercised en masse. The routines were watched by thousands of spectators. Receiving exotic fruits reinforced the perception that we should all be attending such special events, while also experiencing the "generosity" of a caring regime.

The communist entertainment for primary schools included a pre-Christmas gathering, in which children were encouraged to recite Russian poems and songs. All the desks and chairs were moved to one side of the classroom, in order to create space. The festive paper decorations on the walls were pleasing to the eyes, as were all the photographs of the 'great leaders' hanging over our heads throughout the year. On the blackboard, С Новым годом was written in chalk, which means *Happy New Year* in Russian. During the festive gatherings at school, we were often dressed in handmade costumes that represented a specific animal. One year, I remember dancing in circles, dressed as ladybugs and bees. We had to sing in a foreign language, drank tea, and received some fruit too.

At home we rarely ate exotic fruit. Because of our low income, there wasn't a great deal of variety to the food that my family could afford. On Sundays, we ate chicken, and my father bought himself horse salami – which was one of the cheapest and least popular options available. Nowadays, the variety of products in Slovak stores makes us spend more money than we originally intended. Selecting products doesn't feel easy to me. What was once exceptional and scarce, is now abundant. Exotic foods from around the world, a wide range of cosmetics, and modern clothes, have all become commonplace.

At the end of the day, I'm grateful for the products I can now easily buy. They continue improving the quality of my life, but every so often my mind goes back to a simpler time.

Sweet Mismanagement

Children are always pleased to receive pocket money from their parents. For us, pocket money truly meant extra money, as our Mama prepared a daily school snack for us. During small breaks at school, we ate our snacks from home, alongside milk and other dairy products given to us by the school. During lunch break, we ate in the school canteen – which our parents paid for.

The pocket money we received on a weekly basis amounted to *Kčs* 5. Koruna (Kčs) was the currency of Czechoslovakia, and one koruna equalled 100 halierov. This was enough money to buy something to eat or drink every day. Our parents decided to give us pocket money at an early age – I was only eight, and my sister was seven, when we received our first koruna. My father explained to us that the pocket money we received had a purpose – namely to help us learn how to manage money. He stressed that we could either spend it reasonably, or save it, in order to buy something more valuable a few weeks later. The latter option seemed less realistic to me, as I already knew the prices of my favourite food. In the small grocery store next to our school, jarred baby food used to cost Kčs 2.60 per piece, and a white roll was Kčs 0.20 per piece. The rolls were made of yeast dough, cut into pieces and rolled to form crescent shapes called "*rožky*". Just imagine something similar to a croissant, but longer, thinner, and with a different taste.

My sister and I also loved the little pies, called "pirohy", which were sold by a bakery that we passed on our way to school. We walked by the window every day, attracted by the sweet smell, and usually couldn't resist buying the fatty delicacies. Pirohy had the shape of a roll, were crispy on the outside, and filled with nuts, jam, or poppy seeds. I preferred the pies with nutty fillings, whereas my sister preferred the ones with poppy seeds. The woman at the window wrapped each one in a small piece of paper, which immediately also became greasy. Since one piece cost Kčs 0.90, theoretically I could have bought one piece per day. But, there is a big difference between theory and practice. Our appetite was huge, hence we rarely had money by Friday.

My sister was a very energetic child. She would spend a lot of time climbing trees, running, and fighting with boys. She rarely played with girls, since she couldn't have cared less about fashion or hairstyles. Instead, her vitality and lust for life manifested in her passion for food. She was quite addicted to pirohy. She wanted to eat pirohy every day, and it seemed like she could never have enough of them. The monetary limitations were so annoying. On Monday she bought three pies, on Tuesday two, and by Wednesday she was staring at me with large, hungry eyes.

'Please buy me one, please!' she would repeat, standing in front of the bakery window. When I refused, she would just plead harder. Since I'm a good sister, I sometimes bought her a pie. By the time Friday came around, we would both end up standing outside the bakery before school, with forlorn expressions on our faces, and empty wallets.

I am happy to say that my relationship with my sister has always been strong. We challenged each other sometimes, but we always loved each other.

Household Chores for All

The division of housework has always played an important role in my family. Both our parents worked full time, and felt very tired by the evening. Everyone had to contribute, so that we could have a tidy house and food on the table. When my sister and I were very little, we simply helped by cleaning our room. By the age of seven or eight, we started helping in the kitchen by washing dishes, and peeling potatoes and other vegetables. Later, we regularly vacuumed. It seemed that the older we grew, the more housework we were given.

Our parents taught us tidiness, cleanliness, and discipline. On Saint Nicholas Day (December 6th) my sister and I usually found oranges, sweets, and sometimes a wooden spoon in our shoes. The latter was our mother's way of reminding us to behave. We didn't find it funny, as it was the very same wooden spoon that we were beaten with whenever we misbehaved. Obey and learn – this was the way our parents brought us up. We were not used to receiving gifts without feeling that we had deserved them. In times of distress, or when I was feeling unloved, I would often turn to my Monchhichi – a little hairy stuffed monkey, which was a very popular toy in the 1980s. They were originally from Japan, hence the name. My Monchhichi had a bib, and was holding a bottle that one could put into his mouth. I took him everywhere with me.

Our parents brought us up with great humility, and we never questioned their values. However, their parenting style was sometimes quite radical. Once, when we were making excuses for not tidying up the mess in our room, our father looked at us and said, 'You don't have time?' He then entered our room and without warning, started throwing everything off the tables, chairs, and shelves.

'You've got an hour,' he said emotionlessly, and left the room.

Our father's behaviour angered me and my sister. After he left the room, we complained a lot. There was a great big pile of things in the middle of the room: clothes, bags, books, crayons, toys, all thrown there by our father. Surprisingly, we even found cookies and potted flowers in the pile.

We sorted out all the items and started to put everything in its rightful place. However, we were still children, and our cleaning wasn't very efficient; every couple of minutes we played with the things we were supposed to tidy up. We were quickly brought to our senses by our father's voice outside the door: 'Have you finished cleaning already? Soon I will come to have a look!'

My sister and I were never allowed to watch television right after school. First, we had to complete our homework assignments, inform our parents about our day, and get them to sign our little communication notebook, called *žiacka knižka* in Slovak. Every pupil attending primary school had a similar A5-size notebook, which contained not only grades and announcements, but also demerits received from the teachers. Some of the teacher's complaints in my small notebook were about me not bringing a second pair of indoor shoes or gym clothes. Friends of mine kept their notebooks long after they'd left school, and I remember spending time laughing and looking over pages full of notes such as: *When I entered the classroom, she didn't stand up to greet me* or *He appeared to be sleeping during my class.*

At home, our television time was strictly rationed. Our parents didn't want us spending hours gazing aimlessly "into the box". We never watched television before finishing our homework, or before assisting our mother in the kitchen. My sister and I always looked forward to *Večerníček*, a TV jingle followed by a short fairy tale. As soon as we heard the sound of the jingle, we knew our programme was about to begin. No matter what we were doing, we immediately stopped everything, dropped what we had in our hands, and ran towards the television. The jingle was beautiful. Grandpa Večerníček would come out of his house with a lantern in his hand. His dog would wake up, run to the grandpa, and pull his jacket. Grandpa Večerníček would nod in agreement, and the dog would bark. Grandpa Večerníček then did something magical – he lifted his lantern, and touched the sky itself – and the stars suddenly appeared. The jingle was so melodic, innocent, and beautiful. Another short jingle followed after the fairy tale. Sometimes my parents watched Večerníček with us, and we, in turn, watched the news with them. It seemed like they understood our TV programme, whereas we usually struggled to understand theirs.

In our home, chores were part of the daily schedule, and kitchen work was included. Although the kitchen was always my mother's kingdom, I was expected to assist her. My Mama often cooked and baked, and her cooking skills surprised me. She was always focused on what was important, such as ingredients and amounts. Our father helped by peeling potatoes and cutting vegetables, as well as washing the dishes. However, Mama insisted on educating and sharing her culinary art with her daughters. Today, I am quite a good cook, and my sister is an excellent one.

Interesting fact: Slovaks love potatoes so much that they invented up to two hundred different potato dishes! Potato is one of the easiest vegetables to grow, and its cultivation is popular throughout Slovakia. Travelling through Slovakia means enjoying potatoes in all shapes and forms: potato soups, boiled potatoes, grilled potatoes, potato salads, cakes made from potato dough – just to mention a few.

When my mother was on business trips or not feeling well, my father was allowed to take over in the kitchen. As with most things, my father is quite gifted, and can still prepare simple, tasty food without encountering any problems. He likes to prepare boiled potatoes with fried vegetables and roasted meat. When we were children, my father always helped around the house – something which cannot be said of all husbands. If Mama was in the kitchen, he was vacuuming or ironing, or sewing clothes for us.

Looking back, I realise how creative my parents were. Having a low income actually made them very resourceful – they learned how to do things by hand, that they would not have done had the right technology or tools been available. In spite of all their difficulties, they made sure that my sister and I had what we needed.

How (Not) to Teach Cycling

For some families, scholastic education plays an important role. For others, school isn't that relevant. My family valued education extremely highly. However, more important than scholastic education, was the pursuit of lifelong learning. My parents were curious about so many different subjects, and this rubbed off on me. I still remember the interesting family debates that took place in the kitchen, the living room, the car, and even in the garden. Unfortunately, there are countries where girls don't have the same access to education as boys. In our home, education was mostly gender-neutral. Our discussions tended to be more educational than conversational. To this day, my father doesn't just write me emails about his health, but he also includes information about birds he has seen – complete with a picture and a detailed description of the type of bird.

One of the most interesting discussions I can remember, was about beauty and attractiveness. When you are a teenager, you don't want to hear about the inner beauty of human beings, since all you can think about is how to save enough money for trendier outfits. Mama explained that the inner beauty of a person is more important than their outer beauty. The inner beauty determines whether somebody is truly beautiful or ugly. Mama further explained that the way someone speaks and behaves can make him or her attractive. She was right. I've met people that I considered very beautiful right until they opened their mouth; after a couple of sentences their shallow and narcissistic ways made them instantly ugly to me.

After graduation, my thirst for knowledge became even stronger. I was eager to explore new places, meet new people with different backgrounds, and learn about history and architecture. As a child, I admired my parents for what they knew. In the evening, they often spoke about politics, different European and African countries, gardening, or about books like *Nox et solitudo* by Ivan Krasko, or *The Grandma* by Božena Němcová. They even analysed song lyrics, so that we understood the meaning between the lines.

As children, my sister and I were very curious, and we asked many questions. We were not ashamed to ask about anatomy and sexuality either. In spite of their conservative views, our parents mostly replied to our questions honestly and directly. They didn't pretend that sexuality was an alien concept, or that it didn't exist. As a result, having my period for the first time wasn't traumatic; I was aware of what was happening inside my body. It was actually me who had to calm down a crying pupil in the toilets after her period started; she thought she was going to bleed to death, and she had no idea of what menstruation was.

My father not only explored theoretical matters, but he was also determined to teach us practical things, to the point where it could almost be labelled as obsessive. We were taught how to plant trees, catch fish, and assist during tractor and car repairs. My father was the one who taught us ice-skating and cycling. We were not only good, we were excellent – queens on the ice, and fast cyclists on the streets.

At this point, I feel the need to mention that my father's teaching methods could be seen as non-traditional, with a certain touch of madness. I will never forget how I learned to cycle. When I turned seven, my father got me a bicycle without training wheels. After explaining to me about how my beautiful, new, red bicycle worked, he then told me about its structure and functionalities. I was allowed to sit on the bicycle under my father's guidance. He was holding the bicycle while he talked to me. He taught me how to use the pedals, how to focus on balance, and how to avoid falling. After a couple of minutes, I was a crazy little devil, pedalling in the yard of the ten-storey house-block. Feeling the adrenaline rushing through my body, I cycled several rounds, aware that my father was watching. I felt excited and happy, until a neighbour approached my father for a chat.

As I watched my neighbour approach, I started to panic. You see, even though we'd been through the fundamentals, and I was a fast learner, there was one thing my father had forgotten to teach me – I didn't know how to stop. This might sound trivial, but it certainly didn't feel that way for me, at seven years old. I imagined that braking too fast would result in my body flying over the handlebars. I cycled fearfully, several more rounds, in the hopes that the adults would soon finish their chat, but their discussion seemed never-ending. Tired, and with tears in my eyes, I kept pedalling. Being a well-behaved child wasn't always an advantage. I wanted to scream and complain, but I just pedalled. Finally, the neighbour left, and my father turned his attention back at me. Upon realising that I didn't know how to stop, he spread his legs and allowed me to land between them, while at the same time quickly grabbing my handlebars. Looking at the expression on my face, he understood that learning to cycle hadn't been as fun for me as he'd expected.

The moral of this story could be: Don't just learn how to do things. Learn how to stop. Being able to stop at the right time can save your life.

Now It's Your Turn

Did you know that old TV sets, the ones without remote controls, were beneficial for the viewer's health? Since the switches were placed directly on the television, we had no choice but to get up from our chairs in order to change channels. Hence, we would often tell each other, 'Now it's your turn!'

I remember watching many documentaries with my father, whose eagerness to educate us seemed to have no limits. As he especially liked Egypt and everything related to ancient cultures, architecture, and inventions, we watched many documentaries about the pharaohs. However, my interest for Ramses I, II, III, and all the others, considerably lessened the moment I learned about a particular fairy tale or film I preferred. Ancient Egypt suddenly became pure torture.

I have always been fascinated by nature and wildlife films, which took me into the world of my dreams. When I was little, my parents often took me for long nature walks. I really enjoyed the walks along the Danube river in Bratislava. I could look for hours at the trees, the grass, and the flowers on the banks of the Danube. My mother once told me that if she had known I'd be like this, she would have called me *Kvetka* (the affectionate form of Kvetoslava, with kvet meaning flower). We all enjoyed watching nature documentaries; there was no need to argue or negotiate. But, as soon as my father decided that it was time to watch a programme about agriculture, excavators, cars, or tanks, we women always protested. My father never had it easy, being the only man in our household; the numbers were simply against him.

Under communism, watching TV did not always mean relaxation and comfort. The news frequently included doses of brainwashing. We were informed about the progress of the five-year plan, and how well it had been met, in percentages. Communists evaluated not only the results of the year, but also the whole five-year period. There were many different units that were obligated to report, for example: plants, factories, services, and agricultural cooperatives. The main hero of the propaganda movies was a simple foreman – Mr. Kudlička – whose ridiculous invention enabled a factory to meet the plan to 1,052%.

Normally, the "useful" news informed us that 'thanks to an excellent approach', the production target was not met at 100%, but at 100.7%. The news regularly glorified the East, and condemned the West. Even at school, our teachers told us about capitalism, that people were treated with no respect, working long hours, starving and poor most of the time. In the East, we were taught that people lived healthy and meaningful lives.

The prefabricated political trials were especially horrifying. Under communism, people were sentenced for crimes that they didn't commit, or just for "supporting" Western ideals. The court hearings were not about justice, but about justifying predetermined sentences. Forged evidence, lying witnesses, wrong interpretations of the accused's statements – I remember my parents often saying, 'I can´t watch this'. It was frightening seeing the black-and-white records of the trials, with the exhausted faces of the persecuted. The system "took care" of people who were perceived as dangerous to the regime and its values. People were tortured, imprisoned. Their confessions were coerced. The aim of the public political court hearings was humiliation and the spreading of fear.

As a child, I saw fragment recordings of the trial with Milada Horáková, and I still remember how sad my parents were. They were not able to watch the recordings to the end. These recordings were played repeatedly on television by the regime, in order to scare people. I did not understand exactly what was going on, I just understood that Milada was an enemy, according to the people on television. She was a thin woman with tired eyes, hidden behind glasses. She was trying to speak normally, while being interrupted by several shouting men. As an adult, I read about the trial to have a better understanding of what happened during communism. I learnt that she had no chance to win that trial. Milada's guilt remained certain and unquestioned, from the beginning until the end.

At school, certain topics were taboo, so I trained myself in silence and kept learning the nonsense. Early in the year 1989, I was punished for misbehaviour. During our civics lessons, we were told to keep the first page of our notepad free for a photo of our choice. We were given the task of looking for a personal hero in the newspaper, cutting his picture out, and gluing it there. I took my time finding a photo, and my choice turned out to be scandalous; I decided to insert a photo of the American president – George H.W. Bush. This resulted in an angry outburst from my teacher. My pages were torn out of my notepad, in front of the class. I was told to think about my choice, and that I should choose a photo of a true leader, someone admired and esteemed. As punishment, I had to rewrite at least a third of the content from my notepad.

Today, I watch less TV, since I consider many programmes a waste of time. The problem is as follows: I always intend to watch something educational, but end up watching a frightening thriller or a real-life murder story. I used to watch television not only to relax, but also to escape realities that I perceived as too painful. Today, I avoid watching TV aimlessly for hours. I prefer to spend my free time taking long walks.

Life Without a Mobile

A trip to a foreign country or a previously unexplored place can cause a lot of confusion and stress. People are often creatures of habit. As soon as the unexpected takes place, we have trouble adapting and enjoying ourselves. When we don't speak the language of the country we are visiting, we feel lost. We believe that once we have planned our journey, everything will happen exactly the way we want it to.

Today, owning smartphones and other technical equipment doesn't necessarily shield us from difficulty. Reception doesn't work everywhere, and we don't always have the time to find the necessary information on the internet. Not having an adapter abroad feels like a tragedy. Imagine a trip where you cannot take gadgets with you – I think many would feel a certain vulnerability. One summer, many years ago, I visited some of the Elaphiti Islands. I chose not to take my mobile with me, as I wanted to immerse myself in nature, sunshine, and spontaneous conversation, while feeling mesmerised by the seemingly never-ending sea. Most of the time, I didn't miss having my phone, but I was glad to have a camera. Yes, I admit I had moments when I was searching my pockets for my mobile, more out of sheer habit than anything else. Virtual communication is a blessing and a curse at the same time.

In my childhood, and in my teenage years, there were almost no portable gadgets. I didn't have a mobile, or a laptop. My father, however, had a computer that I was occasionally allowed to use. He still has a box full of floppy disks, which store work and house-related information. It never fails to amuse me when I think back to that giant computer my father bought in the '80s, and parted with only recently. The PC dominated his entire working table. Today, on a similarly-sized table, I have a notebook, a laptop, a mobile phone, and a couple of books. Life is constantly changing. Today is the good old times of tomorrow.

When I went to elementary school in Bratislava, organising meetings with peers was very simple. During the week we decided where and at what time we were going to meet, usually it was either Saturday or Sunday.

The fountain at Peace Square in the city centre was our favourite place to gather, and could be seen from far away, in all directions.

When we met on the agreed date, we usually stood around the fountain, chatting for nearly an hour. We would then walk towards the park, often stopping by a grocery store to buy some snacks. Since we were always going to the same places, the ones who were late were able to walk around and still catch up to us. If my parents decided we had to spend the weekend in the garden, we had to accept it. While we did have a landline in our flat, we never called our friends to inform them about our change of plans – they simply knew we were spending the weekend with our parents.

I received my first mobile as a gift when I was around twenty years old. Honestly, I cannot even remember who was the generous donor. The disadvantage of that supersize mobile was that it didn't fit into any pocket. However, the advantages were so great that I didn't mind carrying it with me most of the time. For me, it represented a new world, full of exciting opportunities. This world was faster than the one I was used to. I enjoyed making phone calls and sending texts. However, I soon realised that my behaviour had changed. I was no longer paying attention to the places, buildings, and people around me. Paying attention to my mobile screen made me partially blind to my surroundings. More than once, I narrowly avoided a car that was about to crash into me.

Today I am the proud owner of my tenth or twelfth mobile, and it seems that the phone has become an extension of my left hand. I am never alone in my bed, since my mobile is always there with me. We get up together and we fall asleep together. I read online news, I look up information, enjoy social networking, and chatting with friends. Sometimes I feel as if I should change the pace, and get up with a prayer of thankfulness, rather than with the newest social trends. To counteract this addiction, I spend a certain amount of time each year without using mobile communication. Unfortunately, I'm often reminded of just how difficult it can be, and nowhere was this more apparent than when I visited the Elaphiti Islands.

As part of my holiday, I took a boat trip. This was not particularly pleasant – we were on a small ship, and experienced a storm and high waves. So, it was a relief when the captain suggested that we take a two-hour break on the Island of Koločep. He said we should spend our time on the beach or in a café, close to the ship. I wasn't paying attention; I had my own plan. Walking on the beach was not adventurous enough, so I decided to walk up the hill between the houses. I walked far, until I reached a cemetery situated somewhere on the top of the hill.

Surrounded by beautiful nature, I felt entranced by the view of the sea and its glittery waters. I could not get enough of that feeling of peace washing over me. After a while, I eventually looked down at my watch, and realised that I had only fifteen minutes left to get back on the ship. But the docks seemed so far away. Indeed, leaving my daydreams to come back to reality was not pleasant at all. I reached for my mobile, but it wasn't in my pocket, of course! I immediately started to run down the hill, feeling very stressed.

Halfway down the hill, I spotted an elderly woman, carrying a basket of herbs. I started speaking to her in Slovak, in the hopes that she could understand. She looked at me with a friendly smile, and said something in Croatian – I didn't understand her at all. I kept trying to say that I needed to find the shortest way to the beach, as soon as possible. I was repeating 'beach', 'pier', and 'ship', while moving my arms up and down; I looked like a confused little monkey who had lost her troop. Soon, the woman was telling me the name of the street I needed to walk through. She pointed in a particular direction, I gave a quick thank you, and ran down the hill between the houses. In the end, I managed to make it to the meeting point on time.

Many years later, when I decided to visit the Côte d'Azur, I repeated the "how to survive without a mobile" project. Some days were easier, others were more difficult. Life constantly changes. What was normal during my childhood became a challenge in adulthood.

The Spartakiad and other
Collective Nonsense

Despite the collective uniformity and inherent dullness that is often associated with communism, you might be surprised to learn that in my primary school, the classrooms were awash with colour and expression. Children dressed in multicoloured clothes, made of different materials. Some even added shine to their outfits, by using neon yellow or pink shoelaces. I loved this colourful world, with the only downside being that the outfits and their materials revealed who had a wealthy family, and who came from a more modest background.

Our colourfulness was complemented by our favourite break-time activity, which involved *céčka* – little plastic C-shaped toys, which connected to create colourful chains. We either wore our creations around our necks, or hung them as decorations in the rooms. Most of the time, we were carrying our treasures in transparent plastic bags, because we were eager to either exchange our toys or play a game to gain more pieces.

The game we played was simple and entertaining. Two pupils faced each other, by standing at different corners of a chosen desk. Each pupil placed a C-shaped piece on the desk, close to the edges. The pupil that started the game quickly pushed his toy towards the opponent's piece, with the aim of hitting it. If he succeeded, he was allowed to keep that céčko, and another round followed. Everyone was eager to add new pieces and shapes to their collection, and we spent many of our breaks playing this game.

One area where there was no room for expression or individual colour, was in our physical education classes. We all had to wear identical clothes when attending the school gym – consisting of white gym shoes called *jarmilky*, blue shorts for girls and red shorts for boys, white tank tops, and white socks. I hated my blue shorts, as they were always very tight and suffocating. I didn't have what society deemed an "ideal body", and those shorts made me look obese. In the school gymnasium, the girls exercised separately from the boys. Since we didn't have two gyms, we simply occupied one half of the room each. During the summer, we also exercised in the school backyard. I remember my teacher being very strict, taking physical health seriously, and me being tired after all the jumping, running, and climbing. The expectations were high. Communists promoted the health of men and women – the ideal citizen was strong, hard-working, and willing to defend their homeland at any time.

In Czechoslovakia, we had something called *Spartakiády*. These were collective sports events, that took place at the Strahov Stadium in Prague. They had ideological overtones, and aimed to show the world how good and healthy life in Czechoslovakia was. People wore special attire and performed synchronous exercises, which were quite demanding. Luckily, I could avoid Spartakiáda, but not the other collective stupidities. Communist leaders knew that manipulating children's brains was important, and inventing roles with different levels of importance seemed an excellent way to do just that. It was almost as if they were trying to convince the youth that the communist values were more important than those of their parents.

At first I was a little spark (in Slovak: *Iskra*), and later I became a pioneer (*Pionier*). Being an Iskra or a Pioneer became normal, something that people accepted without questioning. Although at school we practised several elements of the Spartakiads, unlike many other students we didn't have to actually participate in such sporting events, which were an important part of communist propaganda.

The pioneers attended official events dressed in a blue pioneer uniform, trousers for the boys and skirts for the girls, with a red scarf knotted around the neck. The scarf had to be worn in a particular way, with one end longer than the other, to make it appear like the number one, meaning always aiming for the best grades at school. Just try and visualise that. There was also a badge showing the Czechoslovakian flag, a book-chronicle, and a flame. Such nonsense still makes me laugh, even after all these years. Pioneer greetings meant shouting, 'Be prepared to build and protect the socialist homeland!' And they replied, 'Always prepared!' Screaming such words sometimes made me wonder exactly what I was getting ready to fight for. The whole greeting was absurd.

In reality, I wasn't a soldier in the army, just a child standing on Slavín and shouting something I didn't really understand. Slavín is a war memorial in Bratislava, commemorating the liberation of the town by the Red Army in 1945. It has a cemetery, where thousands of Soviet soldiers rest. Slavín was the place where, during the anniversaries, we placed wreaths of thankfulness for the liberation from the Nazis. It was also where we completed our pioneer vows as children. The ones who were about to become pioneers had to repeat the words of the vow:

I promise before my comrades that I will work, learn and live according to pioneer laws, that I will be a good citizen of my beloved homeland, Czechoslovak Socialist Republic and with my conduct I will protect the honour of the pioneer organisation – the Socialist Union of Youth.

Once we had completed the vows, the red pioneer scarves were tied around our necks. Pioneers held meetings and gatherings throughout the school year. Summer holidays were often packed with different activities in pioneer camps.

The pioneer camps enabled us to spend several days each year in the fresh air, surrounded by nature. We enjoyed the camps, as the instructors taught us how to recognise different types of trees, how to orientate ourselves in the forest, and how to survive if we ever got lost. I remember one particularly adventurous afternoon when we were marching in the forest, and an instructor decided to teach us Morse code. The existence of such a code amazed me, and I was determined to become an expert in this. A dot represented a short syllable, and a dash a long syllable. One has to know that in Czech language, there are letters with a diacritical mark called *dĺžeň*, an acute accent. Imagine children walking through fields and forests memorising: A is *akát* (Morse code: dot dash), B is *blýskavice* (Morse code: dash dot dot dot), C is *cílovníci* (Morse code: dash, dot, dash, dot) and so on. I decided to use Morse code to exchange short messages with a friend, who stayed in the same wooden hut. This great advantage enabled us to confuse other children, who tried to snatch our little notes.

I liked the pioneer camps, we spent a lot of the time with nature, singing and dancing. What I didn't enjoy was the frequent feeling of hunger. We were given simple meals in modest portions. Breakfast meant a single roll with butter and hot milk. At home, I ate at least two rolls, and nobody would offer me hot milk, since my family knew that I felt sick just looking at it. My issues with hot milk started in kindergarten, where the carers didn't "care" about my dislikes, and tried many times to make me drink a cup of hot milk with a disgusting layer of skin on top. I often removed the skin from the top, and threw it under the table. Sometimes I even refused to drink the milk at all. I was physically punished for such actions, hit on my bottom, and even slapped on my face. Nowadays, this is an action that nobody would tolerate, but back in the '70s and '80s, physical punishments were considered to be, to a certain extent, acceptable. In the pioneer camp, they gave us such small portions that I had to wait a couple of minutes for the milk to cool down, remove the skin, and force it down. One had to find a way to survive.

Summer in pioneer camps wasn't only for entertainment and camaraderie. The communist regime was eager to spread their propaganda. We were regularly made to attend open-air formations, in our pioneer uniforms. There are many absurdities in life, but putting on a uniform on a hot day, while standing motionless, next to other sweaty children, is definitely one of the most ridiculous things I have ever done. I absolutely hated this activity, but always participated, as I knew it was a must before being able to enjoy the surrounding nature.

Sometimes we do things that we don't want to do, in order to do the things we want to do. The real problem comes when we begin to act against our conscience and our values. If you compromise too much, and too often, you'll only end up unhappy.

The Bird Flies Soon

Photoshoots were always meticulously organised in our school. Group photos were taken at least once per year. In order to have the perfect picture, our parents were forewarned about when the photoshoots would happen, so that they could prepare us. On the morning of the photoshoot, our parents chose our smartest clothes, brushed our hair, and repeatedly said, 'Don't forget to smile.'

In kindergarten photos, each group consisted of up to twenty children, all doing their best to give the assistant a hard time. Children want to talk, laugh, and chase one another. Sitting, or standing still and smiling, just because we were told to, wasn't an easy concept to grasp. However, we feared our nursery assistant, who would make us stand in the corner if we did something naughty, and so everyone ultimately ended up behaving themselves. Shortly before each photoshoot, the kindergarten assistant ordered us to be quiet, looking at us with what seemed like her strictest face. The adults brought a wooden bench, and the assistant chose the children who sat on it. The other children gathered behind the bench. Once all the children were 'arranged' for the photo to be taken, the kindergarten assistant walked behind the photographer, to enable him to take a picture of us, without her. The photographer stepped behind the camera and said aloud, 'Smile, a bird is going to fly soon', in Slovak: 'Úsmev prosím, vyletí vtáčik!' In other countries people say 'Cheese!' shortly before their photo is taken, but in Czechoslovakia we had the 'bird warning' telling us the moment to smile.

The photographer seemed to hope that upon his command, the children would start smiling and look directly at the camera. This never happened. In my kindergarten, there were always at least one or two people who weren't smiling, or weren't looking into the camera. The children who looked serious, or even angry, were particularly funny. Many years later, I met some of the children from kindergarten, whose adult faces showed similar features to those in the photos. Those who were frowning before, are still frowning today. It's quite interesting how children's faces already tend to express their personality traits. You can tell a lot about a person just by seeing their facial expressions.

I still remember that in my first year at primary school, I cried when I heard that we had an upcoming photoshoot. I wanted to avoid it at any cost, and begged my mother not to send me to school. I had been stung by a bee in the proximity of my eye, and my swollen face looked terrible. *A photo is something I will have to keep forever*, I thought, and I was willing to fight if someone approached me with a camera. Fortunately, the swelling disappeared the day prior to the photoshoot. I was left with a little red stain next to my eye, which served as a memento of that close call.

In addition to the group photos, the photographer took pictures of every child standing alone next to the Christmas tree. My parents had a vast collection of pictures, not only testifying to my development, but also documenting Christmas tree decorations throughout the '70s and '80s. Every photo taken at school had its own charm; it showed a moment long gone, in an era with all its peculiarities, like clothes and haircuts. Looking at them meant diving into an ocean of memories, of friendships, youth, and school struggles. When I first started school, my mother dressed me in a white blouse, with a traditional Slovak floral pattern, and a red skirt. A pair of small, plastic, pearl earrings were meant to complete the overall style, but the earrings didn't really match with the rest. Still, I considered it important to wear earrings every day, as my confusing "helmet haircut" made many think I was a boy. My hairstyle simply looked like a hairdresser had cut around my hair while I was wearing a motorbike helmet with the visor up.

As I said earlier, during my childhood we had to wait for everything. It took several days until the photographer developed and delivered the pictures. My parents always paid the amount they were told to. Even if they didn't like some of the photographs, they never once complained to the teachers. While today, in the digital world, we can select photos before development, it was a different world when I was a pupil. We only had one chance to take the photo, before it was delivered. We faced many situations like this, between accepting what was given or getting nothing at all.

I tend to look at the old photos fondly. If there were a competition for the funniest school photo, then I am sure that one of my sister's photos would be the winner. My eight-year-old sister, with her funny, boyish 'helmet haircut', next to fellow pupils that were dressed as lady beetles. Behind them, somebody wrote the Russian words С Новым годом (Happy New Year) on a blackboard.

I'm still trying to figure out the connection between children, bees, and the Russian New Year celebrations.

Do You Speak English?

Learning a foreign language is both time and energy consuming. Unless one finds a good library, a free app, or an online language exchange, learning a language costs money, and one has to be disciplined before they can claim to speak a particular foreign language.

Throughout my childhood, my parents tried to find out where my talents were, and what I would enjoy. My father played the guitar for many years, and my mother liked learning foreign languages, German in particular. So, naturally, they tried to get me interested in foreign languages and music.

All the attempts to ignite my passion for musical instruments failed. Trying to teach me the basics of playing the guitar or the flute didn't work, due to my impatience and difficulties remembering chords. After noticing my lack of interest, my mother told my father that it would be better to put the guitar away, and register me for a German language course. After a few weeks of attending the course, my parents realised that it was the right choice. I quickly picked up new words, and surprisingly easily too. Their six-year-old daughter walked into the flat singing foreign songs such as: "Fuchs du hast die Gans gestohlen" (Fox you have stolen the goose) and "O Tannenbaum" (O Christmas tree). At that moment, my parents knew they had helped me to find my talent. To this day, I am grateful that my parents let me attend the course. Upon completion, I received a doll as a gift, and was beaming with happiness.

Since there were close trade and political ties between the USSR and the GDR, the children in Czechoslovakia mainly learnt two foreign languages – Russian and German. When I was eight years old, I started to learn Russian at school. That was never the plan, nor was it the intent, of my parents. They wanted me to focus on German. However, in order for me to learn German at school, I had to pass a special exam. Passing this exam would allow me to join "the class of excellence" – a class with a more complex curriculum, only offered to the best pupils of the primary school.

Every year, the class of excellence was formed specifically for third graders aiming at a higher intellectual focus. Prior to the exam, my parents were told that I would learn German in addition to other school subjects. Unfortunately, and to their surprise, the curriculum for the class of excellence changed, and we all had to learn Russian. My parents could not hide their disappointment, and I later understood why. They thought that one day, communism would be over, and they considered German more attractive for communication with the West. My mother even said, 'If I knew that you had to learn Russian, I wouldn't have encouraged you to pursue the class of excellence.'

Since Russian and Slovak belong to the same group of Slavic languages, I didn't have trouble with the pronunciation of Russian words. On the other hand, writing seemed to be really challenging. When I first looked at the Cyrillic, I thought that I was looking at Egyptian hieroglyphs! It seemed to me that I would need weeks to learn such a different alphabet. However, in the end, it only took me a couple of days to learn it, because our teacher knew how to teach children through repetition and rhyme. Her playful teaching method included a song in which the letters were combined with rhymes. In the beginning, we sang: 'а б в г д е ё ж – вот читаю я уже.' (Imagine something similar to 'A, B, C, D, E – how clever I could be.') However, some of these letters didn't make much sense, as they were merely soft and hard signs that changed the pronunciation of the letters they were attached to.

The Russian language is nice and melodic. I really liked several songs and poems from the time. For example, at school we used to sing the song "Moscow Nights". This is a song about the beauty of the dawn, of the peaceful Moscow nights. The poems *My Friend I Have Forgotten* and *Winter Morning,* written by Aleksander Pushkin, were particularly beautiful. While many people remember this period, they wouldn't admit to it. They have an aversion to anything Russian, in an attempt to avoid thinking about the decades spent under a totalitarian regime.

While I always liked the Russian language, I never liked memorising Russian texts about the Great October Socialist revolution (VOSR) and the biographies of Lenin and Stalin. I could have happily gone through life without such activities taking up my memory. Honestly, I feel like I had to learn more dates in primary school than I did in university! I consider myself a creative adult, and I definitely didn't lack imagination as a child either. In general, learning new things only increased my curiosity to learn even more. I was an ambitious and stubborn child, who never wanted to say, 'I don´t know'. I particularly enjoyed standing in front of the class and answering the teacher's questions during an oral assessment. The problem was that if I didn't know a word in Russian, I simply used a Slovak word, and pronounced it 'the Russian way'. Sometimes I succeeded, other times my answer resulted in the entire class bursting into laughter, and the teacher looking rather disappointed.

One example of my creative nonsense was the word 'chalk'. Instead of 'мел' (the correct Russian word) I said 'Krida', which was similar to chalk in Slovak. Another awkward moment was when I said that 'the soldiers have a difficult stomach' (тяжелый живот) instead of saying they have a difficult life. In Russian, the word 'живот/zivot' means 'stomach', whereas in Slovak it means 'life'.

After the fall of the totalitarian regime, I started learning English. In my early teens, I considered English very cool, because I wanted to understand the many Western songs that I was listening to. Learning and using a foreign language means experiencing many new and often comical situations. As with any other foreign language, English has grammatical rules and exceptions to those rules that catch us out. For example, many jobs in English end with the suffix -er. For example: baker, teacher, banker, reporter. Imagine being called 'a good cooker' by your friend. Yes, he meant well. And I am a good cook!

I can imagine that everyone who has learnt a foreign language will be able to recall at least one humorously awkward situation or social faux pas. It's part of the overall experience, after all.

Buried Treasure

Many people dream of owning a house with a garden. It often takes many years of work before one can even afford to buy an apartment or house. There are people whose dreams will eventually come true, but there are also those who just keep on dreaming for most of their life.

During my early childhood, we lived in a small, rented flat. Then, when I was about seven years old, my parents bought an old and partially crumbled house, with a big garden. It was situated in a village called Chorvátsky Grob. The name Chorvátsky Grob is unusual for a Slovak village, since Chorvátsky means "Croatian", and Grob means "grave" or "pit" in Croatian. The history of the name dates back to the 16th century, when Croats fled from the Turks – who were ravaging regions of the Balkan Peninsula. The Croats feared the Ottoman Empire, and their fear rose after the Battle of Mohács, in 1526. The Croats eventually began to settle down in the Danube region, and slowly entered Slovak territory. They were skilled in the areas of agriculture and viticulture. Croatian traditions related to music, dance, lace making, and painting can be experienced even today in the village of Chorvátsky Grob. Surprisingly, many of the five thousand inhabitants of the village come from different parts of Slovakia.

I must say, I did not like the old house. The front rooms of our home were, for security reasons, no longer habitable. My father stored old furniture, various tools, and technical equipment there. The small kitchen located in the centre of the house was my favourite room. We spent a lot of time cooking, eating, and debating about family and world issues there. Our guests enjoyed sitting in the kitchen, because there was always something to eat and drink. Moreover, during cold winters, the stove made that little room warm and cosy. This was also where we processed the meat after a pig slaughter.

The cold bedroom, located in the rear of the house, was made a bit nicer by my father, who had to use coal or briquettes in the chimney place during winter nights. The bedroom was a poor man's room. Entering the room, one could see a cupboard and small table on the left, with a black-and-white TV placed on it. Next to the window, that was blocked by bars like a prison cell, was a wall full of hangers. Here, we hung the old clothes that we used when working in the garden and around the house. The paint on the walls was cracked. The floor was dirty. I will never forget the smell of that room. On the right side of the room there was the chimney. In the centre of the room there were four large metal beds, covered by clean linen sheets. Under the beds were mousetraps. The only thing I really liked was a small collage on the wall – a postcard sent from a seaside somewhere in Europe, and around the postcard there were little, colourful seashells forming a beautiful mosaic frame.

As a child, I thought that the garden was huge, but it seemed to become smaller each year. The garden produced a lot of fruit and vegetables. In the best years, my father made 1000 litres of wine, and we harvested around 200 kg of tomatoes, 400 kg of potatoes, and 200 kg of beans. Although we only spent the weekends in the garden, my father also watered it during the week. As I've mentioned, my father is a versatile and practical man, and he built an irrigation system within the vineyard, which could be activated by the press of a button.

Despite my father's ingenuity, there were still areas of the garden that needed to be watered manually – particularly the flowers planted next to the house. During my years as a teenager, I didn't like to work in the garden. This was particularly true during the weekends where my friends met in Bratislava, while I was stuck pulling weeds out in the garden. There were days I felt desperate and angry at my parents, because I simply couldn't understand why they were so strict.

As an adult, I came to understand the benefits of gardening. Today, whenever I return home, I enjoy gardening work. It's great to be able to grow your own fruits and vegetables. Eating your own homegrown tomatoes is amazing. The vegetables you can buy in the stores are often so watery and tasteless; they don´t even have a healthy colour. My parents used fertilisers sparingly, and only took them out of the shed if necessary, especially if we had an infestation of mildew.

My parents have always taught us that enjoying the fruits of your labour isn't the only advantage of gardening. Hours spent in the fresh air are beneficial for both the body and mind. Being in contact with nature helps to heal and overcome many problems. Today we spend most of the time in artificial places (like offices, flats, stores) – without nature, without fresh air. As an adult, I understand how valuable days spent in the garden are. The plants, trees, fruits, vegetables, flowers, and herbs, with all their colours and shapes, are breathtaking. Nature teaches us humility. Even if we spend months planting seeds, pulling out weeds, hoeing, and irrigating, there is no guarantee that we are going to enjoy the harvest. Bad weather and parasites can easily destroy unripened fruits. We don´t have control, even if we want to think that we do. When I talk with people who are closer to nature, I notice that many of them are respectful, humble, and joyful.

In the garden, my sister, my mother, and I usually stood close to each other, pulling out weeds and hoeing. One summer weekend, in the mid '80s, something happened that changed my attitude towards garden work. My sister uncovered a small, glittery object. She picked it up, spat on it, and started to clean it with the end of her shirt. Soon, she began to scream, full of joy. My mother and I came over, to see what was going on. We immediately noticed that it was a very dirty coin. We were quite curious, so we looked for my father to help us solve the mystery. He cleaned the coin with a special fluid, and it turned out to be an old halier coin, which was already withdrawn from the payment system of CSSR (Czechoslovak Socialist Republic). Soon we found another coin, which we carefully cleaned, and put into a coin album. And of course, we were hoping to find more coins after the first two.

Suddenly, gardening became a big adventure for us, and we were eager to spend time doing weed removal. Over a long period of time we found around twenty coins. They were mostly old Czechoslovak coins, which were already withdrawn from the payment system. We also found Pfennig coins from GDR. However, there was a coin which made us very excited after we finished cleaning it – a nineteenth century coin, dating back to the Austro-Hungarian period.

I haven't seen our coin collection for some time now, but would really enjoy going through it again. The album containing our memories remains in my father's care.

Finding hidden treasures is such a joy. Now imagine finding a treasure within yourself. How would that feel?

The Wooden Shed

'Good morning. I'd like to buy two scoops of chocolate and one scoop of lemon ice cream,' I said to my little sister, with a smile on my face.

My sister looked proudly at the different piles of sand, each representing a different type of ice cream. The first pile, a mix of sand and small pieces of wood, represented chocolate ice cream. The second mix, sand and flower petals (mostly dandelions), was "sold" as lemon ice cream. The third pile was a mixture of sand and walnut shells. In our imagination, this was the nut flavoured ice cream. The forth ice cream was the candy ice cream – and very popular too. This was a pile of sand mixed with newspaper shreds. Finally, vanilla ice cream was represented by a pile of pure sand.

'Good morning,' my sister said. 'So, two scoops of chocolate and one lemon? Good.'

Holding her toy shovel and a bucket, she started to serve out the mixture. After putting the first shovel of sand with little wooden pieces into the bucket, she repeated. Finally, after putting some of the sand with dandelion petals into the bucket, she reached out, dangling the bucket in front of me.

I pulled a face. 'Give me a little more, don't be stingy!'

My sister smiled. She took the scooper and added extra lemon ice cream into the bucket. 'That makes 3 crowns altogether,' she said.

Of course, I had my means of payment with me. I reached into my pocket and took out three red stones of a similar size, and exchanged them for the "ice cream-filled bucket". I considered it a good purchase, and in my mind I certainly enjoyed every last bit of that ice cream.

Children often copy the behaviour of the adults around them. Children also tend to use the same language as their parents, without being completely aware of its meaning. My sister and I often played the ice cream game, and the flavours varied with our imagination. Sometimes we happily served our "customer" Janka – the 3-year-old daughter of a family friend.

The wooden shed that we used as our ice cream shop, was situated next to our old house in the village, Chorvátsky Grob. The shed, used for storage, served our needs when bad weather did not allow us to play outside. Dressed in old clothes, we felt free to use all corners of the shed, experimenting with how far we could reach. We didn't mind dirt, nor did we worry about tearing our clothes while climbing over the fences or on trees.

My sister and I had similar outfits, consisting of worn out brown shoes, blue sweatsuits, grey lightweight jackets, and yellow caps. In our childhood years, people sometimes couldn't tell us apart, and without seeing us together they would have thought that I was my sister and vice versa. Since there are only fourteen months between us, and we indeed looked similar as children, I often had to patiently explain who I was.

The world in our shed was filled with many adventures. After each day spent in the shed, our mother would have to remove the dust that accumulated on our trousers, and throw away the small pebbles she found in our pockets and shoes. She even dared to throw away the red stones that we used as currency, forcing us to collect new ones the following day. The shed was a messy place, dominated on the right side by a huge pile of wooden slats. There was also a huge stack of glass plates, covered by a simple metal frame. Most of our dolls, books, plastic moulds, toy buckets, and shovels were spread out all over the place. Our parents sacrificed one blanket, and we used this to create a nice sitting arrangement for us and Janka.

We frequently had to rebuild our shop, as in our absence the wind blew the sand away, and stray cats tipped most of the buckets over. Cats – we loved them so much. But they didn't always love us back. No wonder, considering the fact that we tried to dress them in our doll clothes, pretending they were our children. However, in spite of "all the suffering", the cats came to us because they knew that we would always feed them with some of our own food. Amazingly, up to four cats accompanied us during our activities within the yard and also in our garden. Particularly entertaining were those Friday evenings when our Trabant car approached the gate, and many of the neighbourhood cats gathered in our yard, waiting for food and attention.

My sister and I spent a lot of time with little Janka, playing in our shed. We felt responsible for Janka, since she was very young, and the adults told us to take care of her. When she played with us, our parents checked on us more frequently. From time to time, we even had to show ourselves in order to reassure them. I really enjoyed the time that the three of us spent in that old shed. The never-ending discussions, the laughs, and (ice cream) games were amazing. Still, I perceived Janka to be very curious. She would always ask so many questions, and not all of them good either! One afternoon, she interrupted a conversation between me and my sister. She looked us dead in the eye, and said, 'What is hell?'

My sister looked at me expectantly.

'Hell is a place where bad people go after they die,' I said, without blinking. 'It's extremely hot there due to the fire, and people suffer. If we don't live a good life, we might go there after our death.'

Janka stared at me. Then, she burst into tears, stood up, and ran out of the shed. I tried to catch her, but it was too late – she was already standing next to her mother, crying hysterically. I had to explain to the adults that I didn't hit her, and that I'd only answered a question about hell. They told me I shouldn't have scared her. I looked at them with surprise, since I'd only communicated what I remembered after the preparation for the first Holy Communion. I was sure I'd heard something about bad people, hell, fire, and suffering.

Years later, when Janka was a little schoolgirl, and I was sixteen, she had her revenge. I'd persuaded my mother to pay for a perm, and I was absolutely delighted by the end result.

'Janka, how do you like my new perm?' I asked. 'Isn't it beautiful?'

'Well, to be honest, you look like your blow-dryer exploded,' she said, with a cheeky smile on her face.

Never underestimate the creativity of children. Imagination is a powerful tool. Children don't need expensive toys in order to play – sometimes all they need is an old shed, and buckets of sand.

Peaches and Art

The peach is a beautiful fruit, and I have always found the colours to be particularly pleasing on the eye. In Slovakia, one can choose between several varieties. My father has always loved peaches, and therefore, it was only natural that we should have a peach tree in our garden at home.

Growing peach trees means understanding the process of grafting. Grafting is a technique that joins two plants into one. One uses the roots and the bottom part of a plant, and attaches them to the tender shoot from the top of another plant. The cut is very specific, and one has to have the right knowledge and skills to perform the grafting. The choice of trees is also crucial, to combine the best characteristics.

As a child, my father tried to explain the grafting process to me. I used to smile and nod, even if I wasn't completely sure I understood. I was too proud to repeatedly ask the same question. Father also enjoyed demonstrating the sharpness of the knife that he used for grafting. He said that it had to be sharp enough to shave the hair on one's arm, or amputate a finger when a clumsy person uses it.

While I was shy and clumsy as a child, my sister was adventurous. After several occasions where I hurt myself using a normal knife in the kitchen, my father decided it would be wiser to teach my sister the art of grafting instead. I didn't mind this, since I preferred to keep all of my fingers. Looking back, I have to say that my sister was really good at growing peach trees. During our best years we had up to 1500 kilos of peaches in our garden – and we were so proud. Peaches provide you with so many options. In particular, we always looked forward to my mother's peach pies, and we had regular customers enjoying our Sunhaven and Redhaven peaches.

Looking back, I have fond memories of August, when our peaches would ripen. It was always lovely to walk around the garden, eating whatever was on offer. Of course, there is usually a price to pay for greedy eyes, and certain combinations are definitely worth avoiding – I would certainly not recommend combining peaches and tomatoes!

Climbing Adventures and
Motorbike Experiments

When my sister and I were growing up, my father had a tendency to ask us many challenging questions. Usually, and with a certain excitement, he often answered his own questions – for the benefit of teaching us. My father has always had an enormous passion for details, and sometimes this leads to communication issues between him and I. He tends to explain things in great depth, and I tend to lose the plot trying to follow without interrupting him. This created some uncomfortable moments for me during my childhood. On many occasions, when my father was explaining the different parts and functions of a tractor and a car, I struggled to keep up. Instead of mentioning this, I just smiled nervously at him, knowing that sooner or later he would ask me to help with repairs, and that I wouldn't know how to do them.

My father's talent for the technical and practical sides of life has been visible ever since he was a teenager. From my grandmother, I learned that when my father was sixteen years old, he decided to construct his own motorbike. Since he had little money, he went to some metal dumps and collection sites to obtain the necessary parts. He also bought a few parts which were impossible to get for free, such as the engine. Although I was of course surprised by my father's sheer ingenuity, the main reason behind his actually building the motorbike astonished me even more – he wanted to go fishing more regularly. Since his favourite spot was outside the town, he wanted to make his journeys efficient and comfortable. My grandma excitedly told me that there were days where he caught such a large amount of fish that they couldn't even eat them in one sitting. My father's technical prowess ultimately led him to study mechanical engineering, and this was followed by studies in metallurgy.

My father had always wanted a son, but instead he had two daughters, whom he equally loved, and punished. In this respect, it's interesting how self-perceptions are created at a very early stage in life. For many years, I took myself to be a clumsy person, and therefore tended to avoid many activities, fearing I would hurt myself. Fortunately, as a teenager I realised that I was a left-handed person in a world filled with tools for right-handed people. This realisation helped me to grow out of my perceived clumsiness, and I quickly started to produce original, handmade jewellery that was very popular amongst my family and friends. In contrast, my sister has always been an incredible bundle of energy, and still is today. She was strong, athletic, fast, and always seeking new adventures – you would often find her climbing over fences, to explore forbidden territories. Once, she ended up hanging on a picket fence, impaled by the fabric of her own trousers! We only found out about this when she came home, with a hole in the back of her pants.

My sister was not interested in jewellery or make-up. Upon seeing her for the first time, many people thought that my sister was a boy. To add to this, my sister joined a group of four boys, after proving her wrestling prowess. The boys respected her, which was quite unusual, as the girls were not usually allowed to join boy cliques. It was from these boys that she learnt how to climb trees and fences. My sister didn't think much about the consequences of her actions – she would often find ways to stand on top of tall buildings. Reaching the top, she would spread her arms out and wave at the people far below, causing absolute panic, and rescue procedures to ensue.

My sister's behaviour was a welcome release from the discipline enforced at school. Once small breaks or lunch time ended, we had to sit and wait in our classrooms for the teachers to arrive. Teachers were greeted not only verbally, but by getting up and standing next to our own school desk. Pupils arriving late to the class were verbally rebuked in front of everyone and received a negative note in their little communication notebook: *žiacka knižka.*

My sister enjoyed many lunch breaks outside with the boys, trying to discover new territories. Sometimes they were so busy with their activities in the park and other places, that they were late for afternoon classes. The school warden had instructions from the director to lock the front door of the school building for a couple of minutes, after the bell rang, in order to punish the children who were already late. Said children then had to stand and wait for a short time, before the door was unlocked, and they hurried into their classes to receive their rebukes. My sister was too clever though, and thought she could outsmart the system. She knew that even teachers needed a couple of minutes to relocate from the staff room to the classroom.

The school building was a corner building, located on two adjacent streets. The main entrance was situated on one street, my sister´s classroom on the other. After noticing a drain pipe attached to the roof of the building, running down next to the classroom window, my sister hoisted herself up. She managed to scale the drain pipe, and got up to the window, hoping that one of her classmates would let her in before the teacher arrived. Indeed, my sister was delighted when the window opened, but less pleased to see the shocked face of her teacher.

There is a popular Slovak saying: 'He who is too curious will age earlier.' (In Slovak: *Kto je zvedavý, bude skoro starý).* This might be the reason why my hair started turning grey by my early thirties! In any case, the saying above can be explained as follows: Everything has its right time, and if we don't give people and things their time, because of our impatience, we face situations we shouldn't face. Since my childhood curiosity was sometimes combined with carelessness, my adventures often ended in various "disasters". When I went on an adventure, the whole world would know about it. On one occasion, whilst my mother was out, I melted chocolate bars in a pot on the cooker, in the hopes of producing hot chocolate. Needless to say, this didn't quite work – and my mother came home to a house full of smoke. On another occasion, I tried to peel an apple with our sharpest knife – losing the skin on the top of my thumb in the process. There was blood everywhere, and my horrified mother had to get me cleaned up.

Despite the Slovak saying, I believe that it's important to hold onto our sense of adventure in adulthood. Having adult responsibilities doesn't mean that you can't have fun, or be curious about the world we live in. You only have one life, so live it in the best way you can.

Bloody Traditions

Slovaks enjoy eating meat. Even the poorest amongst us will always have money for cheap salami, and this was something drilled into me as a child. I didn't hear the words 'vegetarian' or 'vegan' until I was much older. In our village, almost everyone had some chickens, geese, ducks, or rabbits, which served as a source for eggs, milk, and meat. Some people even had pigs.

I had a special affection for our rabbits, in particular the brown ones, and my sister and I spent a lot of time next to their hutch. Our father was less keen on us playing with the animals, as he knew that sooner or later they would be serving a much less playful purpose. It's interesting how your viewpoint changes as you grow up. As children, my sister and I would watch our father process the rabbit meat, with a kind of grim fascination. My father enjoyed teaching anatomy, and would go into great detail about the rabbit's muscles, bowels, and eyes. He didn't only speak about them, but wanted us to see and feel. Standing there, holding the eye of a rabbit, I wasn't sure what to think. I was too young to understand the horror of it all. However, with the passing of years, my sister and I have changed so much. We grew to love the rabbits, all of which were named, and hated our father for doing it. Flurry-Fur, Redeye, Spotty, and Redfur were meant to live! Later, after the meat was roasted, I refused to go near it. The problem was, I liked meat, as I had grown up eating it. So, this phase of anger was inevitably followed by a phase of conciliation, then the phase of eating.

Pig-slaughter is a difficult subject to approach. The story below might cause some discomfort in some people, but I think it's important to show the reality of eating meat, and how this comes about.

In Czechoslovakia, weddings, graduation ceremonies, baptisms, and funerals were not the only traditional family gatherings. Each year, many of us met at the grape harvest and pig-slaughtering too. Since this rather morbid tradition took place in the cold months, the weather alone was reason enough to enjoy a couple of glasses of Slivovica (a traditional whiskey containing over 50% alcohol). My parents had rather demanding jobs and therefore preferred to buy their animals from neighbours, once the animals were ready to be eaten. Nearly every year we bought geese, ducks, hens, and pigs. Just imagine a whole pig – a 140 kg pig! It can be quite a challenge dispatching such a large animal.

In order to process the meat, we often needed the entire day. *Zabíjačka* (the traditional pig-slaughter) started early in the morning, with the stunning of the pig with a captive bolt pistol. This all sounds very cruel – and it was. I struggled to watch the pig squealing and running around. The whole situation was hectic, and my sister and I helped only after we were instructed to do something. After stunning, the pig was immediately bled by cutting its throat. My sister and I assisted in catching and steering the blood. Collected blood was used for different foods. The dead pig was loaded onto a barrow, and transported from the neighbour's yard into our backyard, where the meat processing took place. Afterwards, my father used a device to burn off all hair, cleaned the carcass, and subsequently hung it with its back legs up on the tripod.

The responsibility for processing the meat was divided between lots of people. With each year, my father got better at removing the bowels. Meanwhile, some family members and friends were responsible for meat and bacon cutting, others for cleaning the intestines. Since the intestine was used for the preparation of various sausages, it was purified rigorously until it passed the smell test – the smell test basically being my father taking a whiff at it and giving his approval to proceed. Traditional Slovak meat products that used intestines as casing, included: sausages (*klobásky*), blood sausages (*krvavnice*), and hash-and-crumbs sausages (*jaternice*). Pork greaves or cracklings were considered a special treat. Greaves are the unmeltable residue left after animal fat has been rendered.

When looking back on our traditional pig slaughter gatherings, I am often reminded of the '80s, with its flashy colours, unique clothes, and the many hours spent listening to songs on cassette decks. In the old days, pig processing was a family-oriented event. Today, I prefer to stay away from anything that involves animal carcasses and blood.

A Blanket of Kindness

When I was a child, we knew our neighbours well. I spent a lot of time playing with the neighbours' children, while both my parents and the neighbours babysat for us. Sharing was such a natural thing. We gave food and food was given to us. Communism meant a lack of material possessions for many people. Despite our poverty, we shared what little we had.

Over the years, I've been given the impression that poor people are more generous. I've experienced many situations where the less well-off were willing to share, whereas those who were wealthy ignored people in need. He who knows the unbearable hunger and humiliation of having to pick green, unripened apples from public trees, doesn't want others to feel the same pain. He who has experienced poverty, unemployment, oppression, and illness (and is not a bitter person) tries to help others, so that they don´t have to suffer. Sympathy is powerful, as it encourages a helping hand.

As a child, I learned the value of having good relationships and helping others, very early on. When you have a good relationship with your neighbour, things become exponentially easier. We shared our bowl with our neighbours, giving them fruit and vegetables that they weren't able to grow in their own garden. My mother did this often. Most of the time, our neighbours returned the bowl, often filling it with their own fruit, or even a cake made from some of the fruits we gave them. There was one incident where my mother wasn't given her bowl back. When I asked her about where the bowl had gone, she said that she had given it to the neighbour as a present. I instantly knew that this wasn't true, but my mother was generous. She often gave generously, and didn´t expect anything in return.

Kindness has many faces. Some acts of kindness towards people can lead to unexpectedly funny situations. One summer evening in Chorvátsky Grob, my father noticed our neighbour lying motionless on the grass. He ran out of the house to check on him, only to discover that said neighbour was drunk. He couldn't manage to find his front door, so he decided to sleep in a grass ditch. After my father realised that our neighbour was just sleeping (he was even snoring), he tried to wake him up – but didn't succeed. My father fetched a blanket and covered our neighbour's body, in order to keep him warm throughout the night. I am sure that our neighbour woke up wondering where the blanket had come from, but my father did not expect anything in return. To this day, I am not even sure if the neighbour knows it was my father who did it.

There are many acts of kindness that people don't know about, acts not published in the newspapers or on social networks, but that doesn't mean they aren't important. A simple act of kindness can have a tremendous impact on a person's life.

Sea Shells and Partisans

Gardens are places of natural wonder. They are also a place of many surprises. Sometimes we find things in our gardens that we didn't expect to. Some surprises are pleasant, others rather scary. Digging in the soil with a hoe or a spade means discovering pieces of metal, bones, and plastic. Finding a dead bird, for example, can scare you a bit, but finding a dead rat can make you throw your hoe and run. And I did exactly that. My father buried the rat whilst grumbling that it was our neighbour's fault, as said neighbour had pigs and a cow, and rats tend to like barns. My father hated rats, although he was less bothered about mice. We always had such 'pets' in our old house. Since my father distributed mouse traps all over the place, my sister and I had to be really careful about where we played and what we touched.

Of course, dead rats and jagged metals aren't the only thing that one can find in the garden. In the area of Záhorie, where my paternal grandparents lived, it is common to find treasures such as sea shells or fossils buried in the soil. After finding small, white shells for the first time, I made sure that my sister saw and admired my treasures. They were about 1.5 cm, and looked like lengthened snail shells, resembling a Cerith. My grandparents lived next to a sports stadium, in a house they built themselves. Since it was unguarded, the unused stadium offered an amazing place for children to cycle through and play various games. The sea shells and interesting stones I found there were rather heavy in my pockets, but I didn't care.

The green area surrounding the stadium felt like paradise on earth for our gang. Our "peaceful gang of young adventurers" consisted of my sister, me, a distant cousin, and three other friends. Since they all lived on the adjacent street, only two minutes away from our grandparents' house, we never had problems in organising our activities. One only needed to ring the bell and ask. Our gang experienced countless adventures, most of them in the stadium area. We liked the grassy ditches a lot. They served as a basis for our "bunker" games, as we simply covered them with tree branches, wood, and grass we found in that area. I enjoyed collecting the building material, since it enabled me to uncover more sea shells and interesting stones.

The stadium was a wonderful place to play. Once we divided our gang into two groups, we began our game. We hardly ever played boys against girls, as we preferred mixed groups. Since there were only two boys who voluntarily spent their free time with us girls, the division into two groups was easy.

'Who will play the Germans? ... You will!' shouted one group at the other.

'This isn't fair, we were Germans before. Now we want to be partisans!' The other group tried to negotiate.

Obviously, even our games were influenced by the political regime and its constant analysis of the Slovak National Uprising, which took place in 1944. Playing alternatively between the Germans and the partisans, we either defended or attacked the "bunker". After destroying it, we would rebuild it and start another round. Once we'd had enough of the playfighting, we decided to cycle a bit more. Leaving the stadium on the bicycle, with my pockets full of sea shells and pretty stones – these were the precious memories of my childhood adventures.

Little Granny, Big Granny

When someone asks me whether I look more like my mother or father, my answer surprises many. In my opinion, I am similar to my paternal grandmother, Maria. I remember her very clearly: her physique, her character features, and her interests.

My grandmother loved art, in so many different ways. She danced, painted, knitted, crocheted, baked (many of her cakes were little works of art), and arranged the decorations inside the house in an appealing way. She liked all things that please the eyes, and therefore, everything from the curtains to the room decorations breathed elegance and beauty.

As children, whenever we visited our grandparents, we always aimed to explore not only the entire house but also the yard. The yard offered many adventures, as it looked like a paradise full of fruit trees and flowers. It also had a water well, two sheds, a privy (pit latrine), and a mixed manure compost. The sheds and mixed manure composts were not exactly the safest places for children, and our grandfather would often warn us to avoid these areas. However, since children are especially attracted to the forbidden, we regularly entered the off-limits areas while playing hide and seek or chasing games (in Slovak: *naháňačka*).

When the adults were not paying attention, we sneaked into the living room to admire the collections that we had discovered during our adventures. The living room fascinated us, as our family never actually spent time in there. Entering the room and looking at the crystal lustre hanging from the ceiling was like entering a different era. The room, filled with crystal glasses, china, and a female statue holding a fruit bowl, seemed to serve for collection and admiration purposes only. The official rule for entering the living room was the following: you may enter only when accompanied by an adult. In other words: don't enter alone, as you will damage something valuable. Well, as usual, what isn't allowed is particularly attractive and magical to a child.

Our grandma knew how to create many amazing products, and we wanted to learn how to do it as well. My sister and I often begged her, 'Please teach us how to knit, please teach us how to draw, teach us!' We spent many precious hours with our grandmother who patiently taught us how to bake, draw, and knit. I still remember how she used watercolours to paint into my little book of memories. It was a notepad, with approximately sixty to eighty pages wrapped in a hard cover. Many children had such notepads, and they asked family and friends to draw or write into them. Children kept these for many years, proudly showing others all the pictures, poems, and wishes they collected. On the first page of their little book, children usually wrote these words to protect it from damage:

Môj pamätník v úcte majte, listy z neho netrhajte, kto ten zákon poruší, dostane pár za uši.

Meaning: Treat my little book of memories respectfully, don't tear out any pages. Those violating this command will get slaps to their faces.

We admired our grandma's ability to combine different pictures and create her own compositions. In order to avoid making an irreversible mistake on our little books of memories, she used a pencil to create an outline first. Once she finished the sketch, she used watercolours to draw a little multicoloured painting. I still have one of her art pieces – a girl wearing clothes with handmade, ornamental stitches, holding a fruit basket. On the side of the page there are various ornaments.

Another important project for our grandma was to knit clothes for our little Monchhichi monkeys. Those who had this Japanese animal-doll knew the challenge that came with dressing up a furry monkey. My sister and I each had brown Monchhichis, and Grandma decided to knit white overalls for both of them. This proved to be an excellent choice, as the catchy overalls were fashionable in the '80s. The overalls usually had a long zip in the front. Since the monkey-dolls didn't have to 'put on the overalls themselves', Grandma decided they should have a button. In order to create a complete outfit, she also knitted a scarf and a cap for each Monchhichi.

We spent a lot of time with our grandma, and we heard lots of stories about her life, and the Záhorie area that our grandparents lived in. She also, carefully, told us stories about our father.

Our father tended to misbehave when he was younger – his intelligence went hand in hand with an overload of energy and sense of adventure. Grandma often had to speak to the teachers, asking them to forgive my father's behaviour, and think about his future. At that time, pupils were actually given grades for behaviour – and bad grades in behaviour had a massive impact on the future of a child, in terms of further studies and job opportunities. However, my father was different from the other children. His technical wizardry was accompanied by an acute stubbornness, and a desire to see things through to completion. If he had a particular project in mind, then he would make it his mission to finish it, no matter what.

When my grandmother was a young woman, she enjoyed dancing – especially ballet. Dancing and other forms of art were considered a nice form of relaxation and entertainment, but families usually didn't encourage their children to be engaged professionally in arts. Children often heard statements such as:

'Art is nothing you can earn a living with.'
'Dancing is not a proper job.'
'Be a doctor or teacher and people will take you seriously.'

Many children listened and suppressed their talents, in order to follow what others perceived as a normal life. Having a spouse, children, and a regular income was perceived as the social norm.

I once asked my grandma about communism. Her simplified, perhaps even naïve, view surprised me. She told me that life was normal. One worked, took care of the family. It was a "normal process" to be a spark (*iskra*) and a pioneer (*pionier*) during childhood, later becoming a *zväzák* and a communist in adulthood. I asked her if she ever questioned the communist regime, but she didn't say much. I asked her this question after

1989, once communism was over. However, it seemed that she wanted to forget. Thus, I didn't feel like pushing her too much, and decided not to ask any more questions, or confront her.

During our discussions, I was particularly interested in the everyday life of my grandparents. They married after WWII, and lived in modesty and diligence. Newlyweds started with only the basics, and had to work hard in order to provide their families with the necessary goods. It seemed like the difficulty of a life characterised by the lack of material and financial means, actually strengthened marriages. My grandparents built a house to create enough space for bringing up three children. When the boys were still little, my great grandmother, who had been a widow since her thirties, began to live with them.

Married life is generally not easy. Two different characters have to organise themselves and find solutions to problems without constantly arguing. If a third adult joins a household, miscommunication and problems are somewhat expected. My great grandmother had a petite physique – a rather small and thin figure. Energetic till a very old age, she helped around the house, went almost daily to church, and she also tended to have her own strong opinions. After she lost my great grandfather to a short illness, she raised her daughters alone. She never married again. She loved my great grandfather a lot. I remember her once saying that she hopes to be reunited with him in heaven. To this day, I remember her so clearly - a small but agile woman in her early eighties, wearing a scarf on her head, and working energetically in the kitchen. I watched her so many times when I spent my summer holidays in Holíč, where they lived. When we ate at the table, and she said something my grandfather didn't agree with, he would just mumble *maminko*, as a sign of respect, and quietly finish his food. He hated arguments, and avoided them as much as he could. Once he finished his meal, he gave thanks and disappeared either into the cellar or into the garden. Grandpa simply avoided wasting his energy on negative emotions, he preferred to work.

My great grandmother used to confuse us with her mix of sadness and humour. Her sadness could be attributed to the fact that the most important men of her life – both her father and her husband – left her too early. She often said that she couldn't tell whether God didn't want to welcome her to heaven, or if He just enjoyed watching her from above. She was difficult to understand, but definitely a strong personality. As a child, I was not only interested in her persona but also in the sweets she used to hide under her pillow. She usually quickly found out when my sister and I took some lozenges sweets from her little colourful tin. With a serious face she looked at us, pointing her forefinger at us and said, "I know you took some lozenges, how cheeky." Then she smiled. Since our great grandmother was rather small, and our grandmother taller, we invented names for them both: "Lil' Granny" (*stará mama malá*: our great grandmother) and "Big Granny" (*stará mama veľká*: our grandmother).

We spent many hours with our Little Granny and Big Granny in the kitchen: baking, knitting, painting, and creating collages. While Big Granny used to play with us and show us how we could improve our creative processes, Little Granny preferred to either take care of the kitchen or quietly watch us enjoying various forms of art. These moments had a great impact on us. My sister likes to paint to this day, and I used to produce handmade jewellery for many years after. We both enjoy the arts and creative self-expression. Most of all, we love to dance.

Dancing seems to not only be a passion in my family, but a passion shared amongst many Slovaks. I believe that people should follow their dreams, and develop their talents. In order to succeed in life, you have to look beyond the negative words, focus on the sun, and go your own way.

Cake with a Special Flavour

For children, spending time with their grandparents usually means enjoying new adventures. Grandparents tend to be less strict with their grandchildren than they were as young parents with their own child. Once their children grow up and go on to have their own little treasures, grandparents become these unrecognisably soft, playful, and indulging people, seemingly reconciled with life.

My sister and I experienced many adventures at our grandparents' home. Full of life and energy, and unable to sit still for long, we were sometimes a challenge for the adults. Our grandparents kept us busy with many interesting tasks, but they also asked us to entertain them with our art and artistic performances. We loved the moments when the adults sat on the bench in the yard and watched us singing, dancing (with our own choreographies), acting, and reciting poems. Our grandparents made us feel so special and unique – when they clapped their hands and laughed with joy, we felt like stars. Despite this, they were always careful when we were under their care. They allowed us to go outside with our friends, but only in the proximity of the house. We were given wristwatches and agreed on the times we met and how long we played in town.

In our paternal grandparents' home, we had plenty of freedom to move from room to room. We were told not to run around, but we still enjoyed exploring the rooms upstairs, particularly when all the adults were downstairs. Our grandparents wanted us to sleep in the bedroom on the ground floor. It was a well-equipped bedroom, but rather cold, both physically and emotionally. Our grandma tended to keep this bedroom clean and ready to receive guests. A long time ago, our great grandmother had used that room, but upon ageing, she preferred to sleep in the kitchen, on a bed brought there just for her. The large kitchen served as the place for most of the family gatherings and meals. My great grandmother's bed was placed in the left corner, and covered by a decorative blanket so as to look less disturbing.

We children knew exactly which rooms in the house we shouldn't enter without an adult. These were the cellar, the pantry, the living room on the ground floor, and the storage room on the first floor. Still, we sometimes snuck into the storage to rummage through large cupboards and wardrobes, to discover interesting objects like handmade blankets, vases, old appliances, and most of all: clothes. Looking at each other, dressed as fully-grown women and men, always made us laugh. Although we were asked not to enter the forbidden rooms, the adults caught us many times playing there. We knew that our grandparents' primary concern was our health and safety, followed by the desire to protect their valuables.

My great grandmother didn't eat a lot. I was often surprised by her food choices. Since she was staying in the kitchen, next to the pantry, I couldn't have blamed her if she'd been tempted. As a child, I sometimes wondered what I would do in the pantry unsupervised, during the night. It was a smaller room, with built-in shelves that reached the ceiling. The shelves were filled with jars of pickled vegetables, fruits preserved in sugar, jams, and meaty products like sausages. For us, this was a food paradise that was difficult to resist.

The bedroom on the first floor had lots of books, but none of them really suited our interests. Our paternal grandparents had raised three boys, and therefore most of the books were set in the American Old West, and written by Karl May. We often brought our own books and magazines from home. Sharing a single bed, which was placed in the corner of our grandparents' bedroom, was supposed to be a temporary sleeping arrangement, but my sister and I slept there most of the time. We wanted to watch television with our grandparents and stay over – we felt safe and happy with them.

While my grandparents made me feel safe, I do remember that some of the evening programmes I watched with them weren't always followed by a restful night. Once they turned off the TV, my sister and I curled up, and hoped not to be crushed by King Kong or enslaved like the beautiful Angélique. With the lights off, all we could see was a very weak street light shining in through the window, and a phosphorescent rosary wrapped around the statue of the Virgin Mary, placed on top of one of the wardrobes.

Night time in that house tended to be exciting. Our grandfather, who slept next to the window, surprised us several times with his sleep-talking. He often seemed to dream of water, as I'm sure I heard him talking about a lake. Our grandmother always turned to us and said we shouldn't worry about it. However, the most adventurous night-time activities were our expeditions to the latrine, outside the house. They took place whenever our grandfather decided that we shouldn't disturb our great-grandmother, who slept one room over, or when the toilet flush was broken. We needed to use the bathroom once per night, so we woke up our grandma, who in turn woke up our grandpa. It usually ended with all of us walking down the stairs to the ground floor, and from there, using the stairs leading to the yard door. The only light we had was a kerosene lamp, that our sleepy grandpa carried cautiously and never allowed us to touch. We followed him until we approached the latrine. Then he turned to give us some privacy. I hated that smelly latrine, with its uncomfortably large opening. My sister faced a more difficult situation, since she hated spiders, and using the latrine during the night was a total nightmare for her. Our night latrine expeditions were quite tiring for Grandpa, but he quietly endured our agitated voices and noises.

The days we spent with our paternal grandparents were quite relaxing, we usually slept longer than them. After waking up, we quickly ran downstairs to have breakfast. Once we finished eating, we had to decide whether to stay inside or go outside. Staying in usually meant a lazy day reading, looking at our magazine cut-outs (pictures of famous people, fairy tales, and animated creatures). We collected pictures we'd cut out from magazines, and stickers that came with packets of Pedro chewing gum, in order to barter. We enjoyed our bartering and negotiations. 'If you give me the picture of Vlk I will give you Krtko.' ("The Wolf & Rabbit" were popular characters from the Russian animated series Ну, погоди! / *Well, Just You*

Wait! and the mole "Krtek" was the main character of a Czech animated series). We hardly ever paid attention to the pictures of politicians or news, the newspapers were merely a source of entertainment to us.

Each time a pleasant smell made its way to our room and reached our noses, we instantly ran downstairs to find out what was being cooked, and when it could be eaten. As a child, I perceived the staircase as being big, steep, and cold. At the bottom of the staircase hung thick heavy curtains, separating the ground floor from the staircase. As the stairs remained cold, even during the summer, our grandma used them to cool down freshly baked sweet-walnut and poppy-seed cakes (called *štrúdľa*), as well as salty meatloaf cake (called *sekaná*). Whenever she placed the hot baking dish on the penultimate step, she would usually scream for us to be careful.

One afternoon, while playing in the bedroom, my sister and I smelled something nice, and decided to have a look. We both wanted to be first, so we ran down the stairs as fast as we could. Dazed by the sweet smell, I felt very motivated to be the first one to enter the kitchen. Just the thought of eating a freshly baked cake pushed me on, and being ahead of my sister gave me an additional adrenaline boost. Suddenly, I felt my foot sinking into something soft, and I slipped. My sister, who was close behind me, cried out, and my grandmother screamed in shock. I lay on the floor, looking up at everyone with big, bewildered eyes, a mess of damaged cake around my foot. My grandma could have been angry at me, she could have shouted, or looked at me with anger in her eyes. But she didn't. She helped me up, and after checking my entire body for injuries, gave me a hug. That was the type of loving person that she was.

As for the damaged cake, it didn't get thrown away. We didn't want to waste food, so we ended up eating it anyway. Believe it or not, after that experience I never ran up or down the stairs again!

Adelka and the Wedding

We loved to visit our grand aunt Adela, who we lovingly called Adelka. Each time we spent a week or two with our maternal grandparents in the little village of Pečeňany, we snuck out to visit Adelka. She was our grandfather's sister, who lived next door, in the front part of a semi-detached house. Adelka lived alone for many years, after her husband died. I did not know her husband, and I am unsure if I ever met him as a child. However, to us, Adelka was perfect.

She had a shy smile, and was a thin woman who wore a scarf around her head – a devoted Catholic covering her long hair in modesty. Her fragile appearance fascinated me. She warmly greeted us at the door, as soon as she saw our faces: 'Welcome children, I prepared poppy seed noodles (*makové slíže* in Slovak), come and have some.' In our language, she actually said something akin to "come and peck some." Perhaps she saw little, innocent birds in us.

As Adelka lived alone, she cooked tiny portions of either noodles or scrambled eggs. I don't remember her preparing any other meals, and she was indeed a modest person.

Adelka allowed us to play in the yard, and in one particular room. The room was meant to be for guests, but it was very crowded with various pieces of furniture and other knick-knacks. She tended to protect her privacy, and therefore we weren't allowed to enter other rooms. The rear part of the semi-detached house belonged to a family with whom we never had any contact, besides a couple of polite greetings. The semi-detached house looked a bit strange, as Adelka's front section was in old-fashioned white, whereas that family's rear part had a shiny orange facade. The entry to the courtyard was always free, which enabled the family car to pass. Adelka's courtyard also had a wooden coop, where I sometimes went with my sister to scare the chickens.

What I considered as one of Adelka's best character traits, was her acceptance. She knew that my sister and I sometimes played with three other sisters from a Roma (Romani sometimes called Gypsy) family. She never had any words of criticism, and she even allowed us to play near her house. The sisters lived in the neighbourhood, near our grandparent's house. They were the only children we knew in the village, the only children we played with there. Our cousins lived a bus ride away, in a town called Bánovce nad Bebravou. The three Roma sisters lived with their siblings and parents in a modest, little house. The girls were shy and always nice. The little one was about six years old, and the other two were approximately our age, eight and nine. We never really asked them how old they were, as all we wanted was their company. The more people participated in our village adventures, the more fun we had.

I remember the difficulties we faced walking with the Roma sisters through the village. People didn't like to see us spending time with them. Some villagers informed our grandmother that we were playing with them, and she asked us to stop. In general, we listened to our grandparents, but regarding this particular issue we didn't. Romani in Slovakia are an ethnic minority, often criticized for their way of living and behaviour. Non-Romani tended to not socialise with them. During my childhood, I only met Romani people in poverty, living in decaying houses or in shanty towns outside the villages.

One summer day, my sister and I decided to organise a wedding ceremony. We realised, however, that a wedding is more fun when there are more than two participants – so we decided to tell Adelka and the three sisters about our idea. Adelka listened to us with interest, smiled, and asked who was going to play the groom and the bride. My sister and I agreed that she was going to play the groom, and one of the Roma girls would be the bride. All the others were guests at the festive wedding procession, lead by the groom and the bride. Adelka laughed in amusement, and agreed to help us with the preparations.

Adelka certainly didn't lack in imagination. She gave my sister a male hat and a shirt, which I assumed once belonged to her late husband. The bride received a white blouse and a nice veil, made from an old curtain.

Everyone but the bride was holding decorative, plastic flowers to enhance the festive moment. The bride was instead given a small bouquet of real flowers, that we collected from the nearby meadow. The bride and the groom looked ridiculously funny, as all of their clothes were made for adults, so these oversized garments made them look like baggy scarecrows. The entire "wedding game" was amazing, and we only held back from laughing during the "vows", which we witnessed with serious faces.

Adelka thought about everything, including refreshments. After preparing a larger portion of the poppy seed noodles than normal, she filled a big jar with fruit lemonade. The wedding took place in the backyard of Adelka's house. The bride and the groom said 'Yes, I do' to each other and, accompanied by all the guests singing traditional Slovak songs, they entered Adelka's house. In the room for visitors, we all gathered to enjoy the noodles and lemonade, but we knew we couldn't stay long. Adelka asked us to say goodbye to each other – the three sisters went home, and my sister and I went back to our grandparents'.

As children, we were unaware of how unconventional our behaviour was. As for Adelka, she only wanted to see us happy. She tried to encourage the imagination of children, regardless of their gender, ethnicity, or colour. The "wedding day" was indeed a happy day, and one that we came to remember for a long time.

Taken Away

The collectivisation of agriculture in the 1950s was an aggressive move by the communist regime against many people in Czechoslovakia. Collectivisation was a forced change, from small-scale agricultural production to collective farming. The regime aimed to change the traditional way of life, and did not take into account the social consequences of such a sudden change. Many suffered because their land, livestock, and machinery were taken away.

Imagine having your possessions suddenly taken by somebody, without being able to defend them. Many political decisions of that era were cruel, hideous, and not thought out. Joint agricultural cooperatives called JRD (an acronym for: *Jednotné roľnícke družstvá*) were created, aiming to achieve agricultural production that could cover the needs of the population. My maternal grandfather suffered greatly in the '50s. He went through a period where he feared for the wellbeing of his family, after his fields and livestock were taken. The perversity of the system was that, for years, my grandmother had to get up very early in the morning, in order to go to the JRD cooperative to feed the pigs. Yes, the pigs and other animals which were taken from them, as well as from other people. It was humiliating.

My grandfather lived in fear, thinking of how a bad situation could get even worse. His distress became stronger each day, so he began to hide money he earned in different places around the house. My grandmother begged him to give her some of it, as there were five daughters to feed and dress. I would describe my mother's childhood as traumatising. From the stories I've heard, it seems like my mother never overcame the pain of the past. Modesty, poverty, and hard work would be the right words to describe daily life in her childhood village. Since my mother and her sisters did not have many clothes, the younger children had to wear the clothes of their older siblings, as soon as they grew out of them. They mainly ate meals made from potatoes, and most of the time they had to walk, because they couldn't afford other means of transportation. My Mama once told me that she had to walk several kilometres just to go to school in the neighbouring village. She also mentioned that she only had a few pieces of clothing. It was really heart breaking when she spoke about the hunger. The lack of food led to desperate actions, that she never forgot.

Since my grandmother and grandfather were under constant pressure at the time, they were often too exhausted to show their daughters regular affection. My mother was the oldest daughter, so she took care of her younger siblings. My Mama had to learn responsibility and diligence at a very early age. Spending time with my grandma and grandpa made me realise how much they worked. My Babka (grandmother in Slovak) had her hands covered in blisters and wounds. It was painful just seeing them. I felt a deep sorrow each time I touched her hands. I often spoke with my grandmother, but I do not remember much of the time spent with my grandfather. He didn't speak much, and there were no stories or explanations. He also didn't organise leisurely activities for us.

In fairness to my grandfather, both he and my grandmother had led an extremely difficult life. When we came to stay with them, my grandma would cook for us, and keep us occupied with engaging tasks. What I remember most from the time spent with Babka was her loud and honest laughter, which I still consider very special. In spite of a difficult life, she would often tell and take jokes well. There were times where she didn't know "what to do with us", as she didn't want us to work too hard with her, so she sent us out to stretch our legs. Since Babka was concerned with our safety, she roughly organised our walks. When she said, 'Walk to the cross and back', we knew what she meant. The narrow path between the fields provided a pleasant walk, and the cross placed just outside the village was simple, yet dominated the area.

Spending time with both our maternal and paternal grandparents helped me understand my parents' values. I often thought about their behaviour and parenting styles. Frankly, I couldn't understand some of their punishments. After asking questions about their childhood, I gradually came to understand why they behaved the way they did. They copied the way they were raised – either consciously or unconsciously.

What I previously considered as cruel in their punishments, I see now as helplessness in dealing with two small children. All they had was their own childhood experiences, and access to a very limited choice in literature on parenthood. I believe those who have had children become more forgiving towards their own parents, and judge them less harshly because they know that one day, they too will need to be forgiven by their children. My sister seems to have chosen the forgiving path, which is good for her.

After the Velvet Revolution of 1989, I saw changes in many areas of our lives. Agricultural JRD cooperatives had fallen into disuse. After the fall of the totalitarian regime, many people tried to take ownership of what used to belong to them – as did my family. We partially succeeded, but it was sadly a small victory, and one which my deceased grandfather couldn't experience.

Milk and Tomatoes

Children living in cities are often unaware of the impact that nature has on their lives. They have no knowledge of how tomatoes are grown, or how milk gets into a carton and ends up in the supermarket. As a child, growing up in a small village, I feel privileged to say that I experienced the full magic and power of nature.

Every year, my parents purchased little plants and took care of them. They "allowed" the plants to occupy our living room – at least for a couple of weeks. Our living room was often packed with seasonal plants placed in small plastic containers and trays, or in washed yoghurt cups – until they could be re-located to the garden. The plants were given a lot of attention by my parents. They were watered, and the weeds around them were removed, enabling them to grow and become stronger. Mama saved and collected the plastic containers throughout the year. After consuming a yoghurt or sour cream, we washed the tray, and Mama threw it into a box dedicated to this purpose.

At home, we always had a great respect for nature, and we cared for all our plants and trees as best as we could. Although we took care of our garden, we didn't always enjoy the harvest. Gardeners know that danger lurks everywhere: fungus can destroy the root system of plants, animals can nibble on small trees – making them unable to grow, diseases like powdery mildew can destroy the vineyard leaves, birds eat the fruit before it can be collected. If there are too many hot days, the plants and trees can't grow; if there are too many rainy days, the fruit starts to rot. And if "nice" people from the village have access to your unprotected garden, then you end up being a very generous person without even realising it. I always found it interesting to see how people justified stealing. Some would steal from the fields next to the village, and excuse their own actions by claiming: 'I'm only taking what is mine' or 'At the end of the day, it´s actually mine.' I didn't understand what this meant, until I learned about JRD.

Slovaks usually have more than just flowers in their gardens, they normally try to grow vegetables and fruits too. It was like this during communism, and it is still this way today. Many Slovaks have vineyards and know how to enjoy good wine. The concept of "garden", however, seems to be different abroad. I was surprised when someone invited me to a BBQ, and upon arrival, I found the so-called garden to be merely grass, flowers, and a couple of trees. What some people call a garden, I call a green area. When I think of a garden, I automatically imagine an area filled with fruit trees and vegetable plants, maybe with some flowers planted here and there.

The milk I drank during my childhood tasted differently from the processed milk that is available today. Sometimes, my mother bought milk in bottles, whereas other times we had milk from our neighbour's cows. My Mama heated up the milk until it reached boiling point, and after it cooled down, we drank it. She explained that the milk needs to be processed this way to destroy harmful bacteria. The milk we received from the neighbour was quite fatty, drinking it was very filling. I didn't like its smell, nor its taste. Sometimes I watched the neighbour milking the cows and thought how simple it looked. On one occasion, upon instruction, he allowed me to milk a cow. Cows are very intuitive, and recognise when a new "milker" is approaching. Thus, the cow became nervous and tried to move away. I placed the bucket between the cow's legs (in the wrong place, I soon discovered) and grabbed a handful of udder. I tried to be as gentle as possible. Looking back, I am surprised the cow didn't kick me while I was doing it!

Going back to my original point, I believe that when you see the sheer effort needed to grow fruit and vegetables, you start to look at things from a different perspective. Gardening has significant benefits. It teaches new skills, encourages people to work outside in the fresh air, and even reduces stress. Being close to nature improves mental health, and the exercise improves physical health – leading to a longer life. So, grow your own tomatoes, support local produce, and live longer!

The Goose

'Who dropped the fresh egg on the floor and hid the mess under the doormat?!' screamed my grandmother.

My mother's parents lived in a little village, where all the inhabitants knew each other. So, when my grandma screamed, even the neighbour's neighbour could hear it. When our grandmother was angry, my sister and I used to run away and hide. We knew we were not allowed to visit the hens in their coop to collect their eggs, nor were we allowed to scare them – although we quite enjoyed the latter. Still, the trouble we collectively caused was nothing compared to what my sister did, one late summer afternoon.

Our grandparents had different animals: I remember mainly pigs, geese, and hens. My sister enjoyed chasing the geese, although Grandma repeatedly told her not to. When Grandpa was in the house or in its proximity, we tried to behave. Grandma wasn't as strict as Grandpa, and she was the one who organised many of our activities and simple tasks, either in the kitchen or in the yard. She took care of us as best as she could. After raising five daughters and working hard all her life, there wasn't much energy, nor patience, left. Sometimes, she simply gave us a Bible and little pictures with saints, with the instruction to 'read and behave'.

My sister usually struggled with sitting on the same spot for a long period of time. One afternoon, while I assisted our grandma in the kitchen, my sister was asked to sweep the concrete pavement, situated within the yard. Knowing we were busy preparing a meal in the kitchen, she decided to chase all the young geese that were in a wooden enclosure kept behind the house, until she caught one. She tied a string around its neck, so she could take it everywhere with her, like a dog. She quickly closed the enclosure and left, together with the struggling goose.

The young goose unwillingly followed, until my sister decided to climb the fence to show the goose to our neighbour, grand aunt Adelka. My seven year old sister had no idea that a goose couldn't climb a fence like her, and thought she could help it by pulling it up. Since the goose didn't understand what was expected of it, my sister started to pull it up the fence.

She suddenly noticed she couldn't move the rope any more, and the goose was hanging and fighting for its life. Once she realised she needed help, my sister screamed and ran towards the kitchen. 'She is hanging, she is hanging!' she repeated the same words over and over. Grandma and I were looking at her in confusion, with no idea what she was trying to communicate. She ran out of the kitchen, and we instantly followed her. Approaching the fence, we found a hanging goose, dead. We arrived too late.

That evening, our grandma plucked the goose and processed its meat. I knew that she was very worried at the idea of telling Grandpa the true story. After experiencing Grandma's anger, and being frightened at what was about to happen when Grandpa came back, my sister decided to leave the village of Pečeňany and go back home. She packed her suitcase and pulled it behind her. She left the yard and entered the road, moving rather slowly, and breathing heavily. A neighbour saw her and warned Grandma, who found my sister and brought her back into the house. What I consider quite interesting is that at the crossroads, she chose the right direction towards Bratislava. However, there was a little problem she didn't realise – the distance between the village Pečeňany and the Slovak capital Bratislava was about 140 km (86 miles).

The goose story is famous in our family, and the entire tale, including my sister's attempt to escape, has been retold many times during our family gatherings. To this day, I feel like defending my sister, as I know she didn't have ill intentions. She has always been a bundle of energy, constantly seeking new adventures.

Faith

'Do you believe in God?' Be quiet.
'Do you go to church?' Don't talk about it.
'Do you have a different opinion than those who don't go?' Don't say anything.

The communist regime ridiculed religion. Most communists perceived believers to be naïve fools, who were unable to lead their own lives. They regarded religion as pitiful. With this in mind, growing up in a conservative Catholic family wasn't easy. Discipline, modesty, and diligence are the words I would use to describe my childhood. Our parents tried their best to educate us and teach us that everything has value, and that nothing is for free. You have to work hard, to deserve the things you get. We prayed often, and went to church every Sunday, as well as on major feast days. Since we often spent the weekends working in the garden, we sometimes had to hurry to the last Sunday evening Mass.

Faith and religiousness go hand in hand, this is how I feel and perceive it. Faith in God has always been important to me. Even as a child, I thought that there was more to life than meets the eye, and I felt a strong need for spirituality and community. Many Christians were scared during communism. We were afraid of the consequences of practising our religion, and preferred to remain silent. But there were also those who were brave enough to spread their faith, thereby strengthening the belief of their fellow Christians.

During my childhood, we sometimes had Christian gatherings at my Uncle Charles's flat. These were family events. In Slovak, Charles's name is Karol; he wasn't actually my uncle, but rather distant family. I called him Uncle, as it was polite. Charles is a good, devoted man, who does his best to live according to Christian values, and I always found the gatherings to be very interesting. These took place late in the afternoon, as it took several hours for everyone to enter the flat quietly, without arousing suspicion. Together, we watched films about the lives of saints. I was very impressed by St. Francis of Assisi, who gave up all his material possessions to live in poverty, focusing on the teachings of Jesus.

These gatherings gave some of us the chance to organise and discuss about how people smuggled rosaries, bibles, and other religious objects across the border. At school, I didn't tell anyone that I was a Christian, nor did I mention the gatherings. In primary school we had a subject called civics, which was basically brainwashing. Here, we memorised the detailed biographies of Lenin, Stalin, Marx, and Engels. We learned when and where they were born, where they went to school, their teachings, the impact of their teachings, when and where they died. All of this was designed to instil the importance of these "great" men in our minds, and increase our loyalty to the communist regime. To add to this, we were also taught Russian. Russian is a truly beautiful language, very melodic, and sometimes the words come out like a song. However, we learned Russian in a communist context. We learned poems and songs that supported communism, and lauded the leaders to the skies. As children, we were 'thankful' to them, for showing us the right way to live.

As I got older, I became wiser. I couldn't have been more different as a young woman, than I was a child. In 1989, I stood on the street, protesting against the totalitarian regime. I jingled my mother's keys, and hoped for a better life. Today I can speak freely about my faith, go to church, and have my own opinion without fear. For most people, these basic liberties are something taken for granted. I don't blame them for this, but I truly believe that in some way, you cannot really appreciate the value of these things until you've lived without them.

Catholic-Lutheran Family

During my childhood, I didn't understand the problems between Catholics and Lutherans. I didn't know much about the history of Christianity, but I heard rather negative words towards Lutherans. One of the most interesting stories in regards to this conflict, came straight from my paternal grandmother.

As I have mentioned, I was an extremely curious child, and I spent lots of time asking my grandmother questions. Naturally, some of these questions were in regards to her love life. I wanted to know if she had fallen in love with my grandfather the first time she saw him, and how she felt about him after over thirty years of marriage. In truth, she really didn't have to tell me. In all the time I spent with my grandparents, even as a child, I recognised the quality of the communication between them, the respect and care that they shared. However, much to my surprise, one day my grandmother told me an altogether different story – about the man she'd loved before she met my grandfather.

My grandma's first love was Lutheran, and therefore her Catholic family didn't approve. In fact, it caused a real uproar, and raised concerns within the family. My grandma felt unhappy, but didn't want to go against the will of her family. So, she didn't pursue the relationship. After that, my grandma thought that true love was something she would never experience. But then, she met my grandfather. When she spoke about my grandfather, the tone of her voice changed. She sounded happier, and lighter, as if all the sorrow from that first, unfulfilled relationship had been cast away. 'Meeting your grandfather changed everything,' she said. 'I felt so loved, appreciated, and cared for. We married, had three sons, and I love him to this day.'

Sometimes, even if the outward wounds start healing, the physical and emotional scars stay on – a memento of the past. My grandmother told me that she once took her baby son for a walk in his pushchair, and they bumped into her former boyfriend. He looked at her, and at her son, and said, 'This baby could have been ours.' Even after such a long time, he could not suppress his feelings.

My grandma wasn't the only one who suffered as a result of the strained relations between Catholics and Lutherans. Many friends of our family have told me about the atmosphere of disrespect and fear that the conflict created. As a teenager, I asked my grandmother to explain the feud in more depth. Of course, as a Catholic, she had her own view of the situation. Catholics blamed the Lutherans for the division, as the Lutherans rejected key teachings and practices of the Church. Furthermore, Catholics didn't agree with the fact that Protestant pastors could marry, thus not taking the vows of celibacy. For Catholic priests, it's important to overcome the desires of the flesh. The reality is that, as with most conflicts, there were two sides to the story. Both Catholics and Lutherans lacked respect and understanding for each other. Most people didn't know much about the Reformation, and they didn't question the acts of the Catholic Church over the centuries.

The history of Lutherans in Slovakia is interesting, and goes back to the 16th century, when the Reformation started. Lutheranism reached the area of present-day Slovakia, and then spread, despite orders that people confessing Lutheran ideas would be killed. Over the centuries, the Church of the Augsburg Confession had experienced both good and bad periods. The Counter-Reformation and the equalisation of churches that followed had a strong impact on people and the ways they could, or couldn't, show their faith. As for the 20th century, the churches suffered for many years under the communist regime. Many clerics, priests and nuns were oppressed and persecuted, as the totalitarian regime aimed to destroy any expression of religiousness and devotion. The period between 1948 to 1989 brought many difficulties for all religious communities.

Today in Slovakia we speak about "ecumenism", with the aim of focusing on what connects us, not what separates us. Although Slovakia is predominantly Roman Catholic, its citizens belong to various Christian communities. There are Lutherans, Greek Catholic, Orthodox Christian, and others. There is also a Jewish community, which is rather small and consists of the survivors of the horrors from the Nazi era, and Atheists have their initiatives too.

Because of the spread of different denominations, it's fair to say that people are much more accepting today. For example, my aunt is Lutheran, and nobody from our family has an issue with this. She is a lovely person, a caring wife, a mother, and grandmother. Our family members respect her and enjoy her company. Unfortunately, back in the '70s, when my auntie and uncle started dating, things weren't always quite so straightforward. My grandmother, despite her painful past, didn't approve of the relationship. With her unfriendly behaviour and attitude, she made the life of my auntie quite difficult. My grandmother went through several stages in this respect, including anger, lecturing, and helplessness. However, ultimately, love triumphed in the end. My grandmother found acceptance. Not only did my uncle marry my auntie, but she became a beloved member of our family. I still remember how she accompanied and took care of my fragile and sick grandma, during my grandma's final years. They spoke and laughed together, while my auntie was cutting and dying my grandma's hair, or taking care of my grandma's make-up. My grandma even asked my auntie what she thought about her outfit for a particular day. Love is indeed powerful, and it really can reshape our lives.

Blame Games

You might be surprised to learn that during communism, we generally went to church without any problems. While secret Christian gatherings were essentially illegal, quietly attending church services was, to a certain extent, tolerated by the regime. The reason for this was that communist spies could easily enter and see what was happening during the worship. Organising religious gatherings in flats was considered suspicious, as they could have motivated people to start a movement against the regime.

All that being said, attending church on a regular basis doesn't automatically mean that one is a good Christian. For many years, I thought that attending Holy Masses was the basis of a good Christian life. However, life has taught me that going to church every Sunday, as well as on all Christian holy days, doesn't guarantee the kindness of a loving heart – because not every Christian behaves Christ-like.

Catholics do not only attend Holy Masses in church, they also regularly confess their sins to obtain absolution. The sacrament of Penance plays an important role in Christianity. Roman Catholics enter a small room, called a confessional booth, to confess individually in the presence of a priest. The priest himself doesn't have the power to forgive sins, only God does. Through the absolution communicated by the priest, God forgives sins, and the penitent is reconciled with the Church.

During my early teenage years, my confessions often resulted in me crying, and feeling fearful – the priests could sometimes speak quite harshly, which was damaging for those already feeling vulnerable after confessing their "most intimate secrets". The sad truth is that some of the harsh words I've received were a reaction to me confessing masturbation. According to the teaching of the Church, this is a terrible act. Sexuality is morally disordered when sought for itself, isolated from the purposes of procreation and unification of married couples.

Today, I experience confession in the Anglican Church, and have come to prefer it. Confession and absolution are part of community worship. Services with the Holy Eucharist include a general confession, said together by all present worshipers, followed by a silent prayer and general absolution by the priest. The confession by all the worshipers, reading words of repentance from the screens placed around the church, is so different from the partially traumatic confessions of my childhood.

Growing up in a conservative Catholic family wasn't easy. On the one hand, I respected my parents, as they often didn't "swim with the stream", despite others around them following it without question. My parents were true to their values and beliefs. On the other hand, I had problems doing everything they asked me to. Daily bans and orders felt like growing up in a military camp. They wanted me and my sister to become strong adults. Though their intentions were good, their educating methods weren't always to our benefit. They tried to demonstrate a strong family unit to the outside world, but there was a considerable difference between the behaviour shown on the street, and what went on within the four walls of our flat. What you wouldn't do outside, you do at home, and the arguments and insults caused a lot of pain.

My mother was quite emotionally reserved. During my childhood, she rarely hugged or kissed us. My father on the other hand, is a man of extremes. Just as he was capable of holding and hugging us for a long time, so too could he physically punish us with no regret. Both my parents had extremely complex personality traits, and each of them had a clear opinion on how things should be done. Meeting halfway would mean compromise, which they didn't like.

Some of the arguments didn't make any sense. They began as a discussion about the programme we had for a particular day. I remember words about where to go, and what to buy, suddenly becoming a wild argument – which later turned into a scene where my mother was threatening my father with divorce. I remember another verbal fight in the car, when my mother suddenly tried to open the car door while we were on the highway. Accusations and blame sometimes led to vulgarisms, which were surprising for us children, as we were usually punished for saying vulgar words. My parents' arguments, however, hardly ever led to physical violence.

When our parents were having an argument, my sister and I would often quickly leave the room and cry in our bedroom. We were afraid to leave our room, as the situation was tense even after the argument ended. As my mother reacted to similar issues in different ways, I was afraid to approach her after an argument. For example, if I came home later than agreed, and she was angry, I would apologise – before waiting a while to ask about food. On some occasions she would react normally, but at other times she would react with anger, 'Eat and do whatever you want! I don't have your respect anyway!' Just a simple question could result in an aggressive response. What was particularly stressful was her tendency to misinterpret what was said, seeing a negative meaning in everything. This was quite exhausting for everyone involved, and not knowing how she would react often made me feel extremely anxious. With this in mind, it's fair to say that I grew up with feelings of emotional and physical detachment. I longed for my mother's affection, for her hugs and kisses, but such everyday emotional expressions weren't something that she could give.

Luckily, I had my sister. She experienced similar emotions and sadness, so we were glad to have each other's support. For many years we shared the same room, slept in our bunk beds, and talked late into the evening. We shared many thoughts, sometimes climbed up or down the bunk bed to sit together and hug each other, or complain if something bad had happened. The helplessness that I felt as a child came to affect my relationship with other people, as well as with God. My prayers were often filled with blame: 'God, why did you allow this to happen?' or 'God, why are you watching this without doing anything?' I also tried to "bargain" with God – 'God, if you do this for me, I will do that for you.' I enjoyed sitting in the church after Mass ended, because I liked the silence. Being by myself and not surrounded by other people made me feel calmer. As I often stayed in the church after Mass, my family humorously called me 'the holy bones'.

With the lack of emotional affection at home, and the perceived radio silence from God, I started to struggle at an early age. My mental problems began sometime around the age of twelve. I didn't value myself enough, and I struggled inside of my head, as well as with my body. I didn't know why I had been given life, nor did I know what to do with it. A blurred identity and lack of self-esteem caused me several difficulties, and impacted my decision-making. From which after-school courses to attend, to the clothes I should wear, I didn't know what to do. Confusion led to sadness, sadness to depression, depression to anorexia, until it all culminated in a suicide attempt.

My internal torment lasted for years. Looking back, I can see one main problem. When someone experiences suffering and anxiety over a long period of time, they may mistakenly think that this is just the way life is: pain and suffering, nothing else. The truth is that emotionally unstable environments can create emotionally unstable people. After years of struggling emotionally, friendship and love helped me to see life differently. One of the most important people in my life is a nun – Sister Judith. If you ever have the good fortune to meet this woman, you will remember it for the rest of your life. I still remember many of our discussions. I opened myself up, and with the passing of time my inner wounds started to heal. I experienced a lot of the closeness that was missing in my childhood. Judith gave me many words of encouragement, she hugged me and let me feel that I was wonderful. The years of our friendship contributed to my self-esteem, and changed the way I perceived life.

Today, my prayers aren't filled with "blame" or "negotiation attempts". Instead, they are prayers of thankfulness for being alive and for the time spent with Judith. We can choose whether to live a life in fear and restlessness, or to live a joyous one. Every person has the right to feel hurt or disappointed, and in small doses this is a natural human emotion, but nurturing negative feelings can only cause more and more pain. We can easily become stuck playing the blame game, accusing each other for as long as we live, wasting our lives in the process. Or, we can improve our lives, through forgiveness. The choice is ours to make.

Radio

The dissemination of information during communism was very organised. The state controlled media and all information was censored prior to dissemination. Total control served as an expression of totalitarian rule. The speeches had to be pre-approved. All literary texts were censored too.

At that time, nobody was allowed to protest. People were manipulated daily. If you were told 'This is the truth, and that is a lie', you were not expected to question it. You were expected to go with the flow, dressing and behaving uniformly. People knew that deviation from the given behavioural and value models meant putting their own lives in danger. Each person could have been prosecuted, with no fair, objective defence. There were even cases where people disappeared one day, and never returned. After gentlemen from the secret police service ŠtB, *Štátna bezpečnosť*, identified opponents to the regime, they investigated, interrogated and, if necessary, "removed" that person.

When I was little, my parents told us repeatedly to be careful at school. We shouldn't be chatty and focus on learning instead. They explained to us that being Christians was a private matter, and we had to keep it that way. Our parents hid many of their activities from us and refused to answer our questions, saying 'you shouldn't be nosy'. At the time, we were cross with this, but as we got older we came to understand why they did it. They were trying to protect us. My parents knew that a slip of the tongue at school, in the classroom, the hallways, or the pioneering or sporting clubs, could result in serious consequences. Our parents were actually very good at hiding their intentions. For example, in 1988, our father attended the Candle demonstration, without us finding out until afterwards. Our parents discussed issues in a way that we could not understand, and deliberately so. Sometimes they waited until we were in bed to organise urgent matters. I remember hearing them talk late in the evening, but their voices were just a low mutter, unintelligible to the ears of a small child.

Mama usually listened to the radio while cooking in the kitchen. We had a rather small radio, which was unsophisticated and cheap, and suffered from frequent signal problems. However, this didn't deter my mother from listening to what the state had to communicate to the citizens of Czechoslovakia. Later, we had a large silver cassette player, which also functioned as a radio. While my sister and I were particularly interested in pop music, our parents preferred to listen to the spoken word. Often, I did not understand what they were listening to. My sister and I were only interested in music. We wanted to dance, to be full of emotion and life, and the intense silence that came when our mother and father were listening to the radio was a mystery to us. One day, I asked my mother about it. Her response came quick, 'Ssh, ssh do not disturb me now!' It wasn't until 1989 that I learned what Mama was trying to listen to – Radio Free Europe.

Radio Free Europe was created to communicate with people in countries with no free flow of information, and to protest and fight against communist manipulation. The station kept people up to date with events happening in countries where communists committed unjust acts and censored information. The station had headquarters in Munich, and people from Czechoslovakia secretly listened to it. It helped them to understand the communist machinations and cruelty. Listening to the radio brought many dangers, as the walls had ears, and traitors waited for the right moment to report their neighbours. Therefore, my parents listened to the radio in an almost breathless silence, for fear of anyone catching them out. As I later learned, my parents' behaviour was typical of the people who listened to such stations. The basic rule was that if you wanted to survive, you had to be ordinary, and invisible.

Candles and Water Cannons

'First you finish school, then you fall in love. You marry, have children, and you lead an orderly life.' When my parents told me and my sister about what it meant to live a good, normal life, they were only doing what they thought was best for us. However, although they talked about living a normal life, a normal life is something they never had. They made their own lives more difficult, since they refused to join the Communist Party. People who had their own opinions were not popular with the communists. Since my parents were Christians, they put a lot of effort into raising us with Christian values and traditions. Faith is important in my life – and not just because I grew up regularly attending church; I have faith because I decided that this is what I wanted. It was a conscious decision. It's interesting hearing people say that faith is more emotional than rational. I think that one does not exclude the other – I believe in God, and it is a conscious decision for me. I practice my faith, and yes, in church or at religious gatherings, I also experience powerful, emotional moments.

In my parents' house, life was about modesty, hard work, sharing, and religion. To this day I remember the lack of material possessions. The deficit was painful, since it was not only material things that we lacked, but a lack of emotion too – of affection and feeling. For my parents, it was important to provide their children with only the necessary, rather than to buy things that they desired. I remember them telling us: 'There is nothing special about us, there is nothing special about you. We were given average talents, so were you. Do your best with what you've got.'

Today, looking back, I have to laugh at the old me, envying my classmate for her jeans.

Although by modern standards my parents' behaviour might seem a little harsh, defying the totalitarian regime had a negative impact on their wellbeing. They tried to be strong, so that nobody could humiliate them, and this mean closing themselves off emotionally. I too felt the dangers of the totalitarian regime, particularly on the 25th March 1988. This was when my father attended a peaceful demonstration in Bratislava, organised by believers who were asking for respect of human rights and for freedom of religion. I remember the feelings of fear and tension surrounding me that day. As my primary school was situated next to the police head office in Bratislava, I saw many officers gathering and preparing in the courtyard. I didn't understand what was happening, but seeing so many police officers, all with serious faces, was scary. I learnt later that evening that they were preparing for a violent crackdown on the people standing on Hviezdoslav Square. During the demonstration, people were holding candles and praying. Despite being peaceful, many were beaten by the policemen, with batons and bare fists. Water cannons with ice cold water were used to frighten and humiliate people. The police screamed at the demonstrators, demanding that they leave. My father was there, defending Christianity, and left the square soaked and shivering. As soon as he came home, he passionately told my mother about what had happened.

Later, I learned that my mum was very brave, as she was the one who suggested to attend the demonstration in the first place. My father had insisted that he would go instead – for her, for our family. Still, my mother couldn't sit inactive, and during the demonstration she anonymously called the police and told the policeman picking up the phone not to attack 'their own sisters, brothers, parents and grandparents.' What she did was dangerous, since all incoming calls were recorded to find out who had contacted the police. My parents were unaware of their uniqueness. I don't know why they said there is nothing special about them, or about us. I can clearly see the uniqueness in every member of my family.

A Beautiful Voice

November 1989 was a very cold month. It was freezing, and my mother, my sister, and I were standing for many hours on the SNP Square in Bratislava. We were shivering, but hope kept our hearts warm. We believed that the end of communism in Czechoslovakia was possible. I was thirteen years old, and I felt so tiny in this huge crowd – excluding my sister, everyone around me was taller. On the SNP Square (in Slovak: Námestie SNP, meaning *Slovenské národné povstanie* – The Slovak National Uprising in 1944) there were thousands of people listening to the speakers in front of us. We were singing, and jingling keys, in the hope to be heard and not to be beaten, or worse. We knew that we were risking a lot. The brutal police attacks on peaceful demonstrators during the Candle Demonstration in March 1988 were still fresh in our minds.

That evening, it was snowing, and the entire square was soon covered in white. We stood there, hoping for freedom. We did not want the regime to tell us how to live, what to believe in, or who to sing about. Even as a child, I knew about the injustice and cruelty that was taking place, as my parents had explained some of the events – to help me distinguish between good and evil. Therefore, standing in the snow, jingling my mother's keys, I was fully aware of the importance of that day. Yet still, I was afraid. He who swims against the current does not have an easy life.

After a while the crowd started singing, 'We promised each other to love, we promised to tell the truth.' I looked around me. Everybody was singing: children, teenagers, adults, and the elderly. I will never forget the beautiful voice of the man who stood just a few metres away from me. His voice, full of strength, provided me with a bit of warmth. I turned to my mother and said, 'Mama, that voice is wonderful.' My Mama smiled at me and responded, 'No wonder you like the voice. It's Maestro Dvorský (a famous Slovak opera singer).'

At the end of 1989, while many people abroad enjoyed amazing hit songs by Phil Collins and Roxette, many Slovaks and Czechs were singing revolutionary songs on the squares hoping for a better tomorrow.

Everyone Likes Ice Cream

I don't like ice cream, and I never have. I don't remember the last time I ate it, but I remember a situation from years ago, when my nephew and niece "forced me" to have some with them. Standing inside a store, they both looked at me, with their big, surprised eyes: 'Auntie, you can´t enter the ice cream store without buying an ice cream, it makes no sense.'

Although I tried to explain that we went into the store only because of them, there are situations when you start to speak and instantly realise that you won't achieve anything with your words. So, I simply bought one portion of ice cream, in a waffle cone, and pretended to enjoy it. There are so many things we do for those we love. Ice cream is a sweet, cold beast. I love cakes, cookies, chocolate, you name it – but my taste buds and my teeth simply cannot handle ice cream. The majority of people seem to struggle with this. When I say that I don't like ice cream, and therefore have no favourite flavour, people tend to stare at me. 'This is not possible,' they say, 'everyone likes ice cream!' Once, I even heard, 'What's wrong with you?!' to which I replied, 'Nothing is wrong with me. It's just the fact that I was born on Saturn, and we have different preferences there.' Replying with humour does help sometimes. Well, believe it or not, when compared with the world today, growing up in a totalitarian regime with all its absurdities, feels like time spent on another planet.

I still remember the first time I travelled to Austria, after the end of communism. I was a fourteen-year-old girl, shy and surprised by many new, unseen things. Although the distance between the towns Hainburg an der Donau and Bratislava amounts to only about 12 km, Austria and Czechoslovakia couldn't have been more different. Where Czechoslovakia had suffered under communist rule, Austria had enjoyed many years of democracy. For me, it was unimaginable that the two countries were once part of the Austro-Hungarian Empire. Since I grew up in poverty, I was also surprised to see all the wealth in Austria.

Austria has one of the highest standards of living in the world, with happy citizens, beautiful family houses, excellent infrastructure, and top-notch services. That being said, I was less pleased during my initial chats with the Austrian people. Many assumed I didn't know anything about the West, and were therefore eager to explain to me what a microwave, pistachio nuts, and other important things were. But superfluous explanations of things I already knew about weren't the only problem. The Austrian German spoken on the streets was difficult to understand. The German I had learned didn't really help. What was particularly useless was the following sentence, that we learnt at school: 'Bitte sprechen Sie langsam und deutlich.' (Please speak slowly and clearly). I wouldn't say that to a person I have never met before. So, I learned a new sentence instead: 'Können Sie das bitte wiederholen?' (*Would you repeat what you said please?*)

To my surprise, people didn't really greet each other with 'Guten Tag', but rather with 'Grüß Gott' (*May God bless you*), and most foreigners could only wonder about how religious Austrians were. Of course, I didn't hear such greetings at school, as teachers in Czechoslovakia wouldn't mention God in their classrooms. Later on, once I made friends in Austria, I came to understand that it was considered a common greeting, and it wasn't really used in a religious context. I was told it's just their way of saying hello.

The border control around Czechoslovakia, and the Iron Curtain, created not only a physical but also a psychological barrier. Because of the barbed wires, Slovaks and Czechs didn't have the opportunity to get to know their neighbours from "the West". Once the walls were down, we started to interact with each other, but those that came from a regime sometimes suffered from an inferiority complex. Personally, I was lacking self-esteem, and felt insecure. What was common in Austria was unusual and exceptional for us. Those who had lived for a long time in democracy, couldn't understand those who'd had to live in another, harsher system.

Visiting the picturesque town of Hainburg for the first time, with its beautiful houses, windows decorated with geraniums, and expensive cars, really made me feel the lack of material goods during my childhood. I thought of our little flat in Bratislava, the old and partially destroyed house in Chorvátsky Grob, our blue Trabant car – it all felt so sad, so unjust. My parents were educated and hard-working, and yet even after many productive years, they had so little.

I've experienced many extremes in my life so far, and I tend to disagree with people when they claim: 'What doesn't kill you makes you stronger.' Sometimes our experiences won´t kill us, but they do traumatise us. It can be difficult to live life without thinking back on the past, and of times when we felt different and devalued by others.

Today, I am aware of my uniqueness, and I do not necessarily mean my aversion to ice cream. I have my own tastes and my personal opinions. Whether it is food or lifestyle, I do not like it when people try to force me into things. Authentic people have values and morals that remain constant. Authenticity is about living with confidence, but still being open to new ideas, and open to other people's opinions. The more respectful of other's views we are, the more we can learn from them, improving and growing as individuals.

Langenlois

I will never forget the two years I spent in the Austrian town of Langenlois. After the Velvet Revolution in 1989, we started to attend the Catholic primary school of Saint Ursula in Bratislava. For me, this was the final year of my elementary education, and for my sister, the last two years. Our parents preferred for us to attend a Catholic school. My everyday environment changed considerably. Instead of pictures of communist leaders, the walls were decorated with images of saints and wooden crosses. The new school environment with Roman Catholic (RC) nuns, dressed in habits, felt surreal. However, once I experienced the atmosphere on the first day of school, this strange land became a very friendly one.

The religious order of St. Ursula belongs to the congregation founded by St. Angela Merici. Ursulines are known for educating girls and women. The 1950s in Czechoslovakia were particularly difficult not only for Ursulines, but for all clerics. Forced to close their convents, they worked in factories, in nursing homes, and as caretakers for disabled children. Activities related to the education of young people were resumed in 1990, by the opening of the primary school of St. Ursula in Bratislava.

At school, I enjoyed learning geography, chemistry, religion, and English. Although I mostly enjoyed Christianity as a subject, I didn't like the Confirmation preparation; it was rather annoying. I remember having a prep meeting with a priest, who sent me away to study more, as I couldn't recite the Holy Days of Obligation on which Catholics are expected to go to church. I definitely didn't miss learning details about the lives of Lenin and Stalin, but what a joy it was to learn about St. Francis of Assisi and St. Angela Merici. As mentioned before, chemistry was one of my favourite subjects. Even my teacher noticed my enthusiasm for organic chemistry, and therefore she enrolled me in the local chemistry competition. My unsuccessful participation didn't discourage me to try to learn more and more.

The final year I attended at the Catholic school was joyous, as I made many new friends. Towards the end of the year, we all had a huge surprise.

Franciscan RC Sisters, from the Austrian town of Langenlois, visited our primary school with a very generous offer. They offered the best pupils a chance to attend their two-year commercial vocational school. The Franciscans intended to cover most of the expenses related to the studies in Langenlois, although parents were encouraged to make at least a minimum monthly contribution (they agreed upon the sum they could afford). To this day, I think it's amazing that the Franciscans were so determined to help young people from a rather poor country. They enabled pupils from former Czechoslovakia to attend their school for many years, and that act of kindness is something I will never forget.

The education of children played an important role in both Franciscan's and Ursuline's RC orders. A great desire to help young people and serve different communities connected them. The day the Franciscan nuns came to our primary school for a visit, several parents were invited to attend the official gathering. The Franciscan Sisters introduced themselves, and communicated to us their educational offer and support. We children were excited and confused at the same time. Since we were in our early teens, most of us had never spent more than a week abroad. More than that, we didn't really know much about life in "the West".

I was one of the girls invited to Langenlois, and my parents discussed all the pros and cons that evening. Their worries focused on my young, inexperienced soul. When it came to my safety, they didn't waste a thought, since they knew that the RC boarding schools offered a safe environment. They were convinced that education in Austria was going to contribute to a better future. They asked me if I wanted to go, and I said yes. After a long discussion in the kitchen, my parents finally agreed on my stay abroad. And so, there it was. I was off to Austria – a new, exciting, and unexplored world.

Langenlois is situated in the Austrian state 'Lower Austria', about an hour's car journey from Vienna. The town, and the surrounding area, are renowned for their wine production. Langenlois, with its vineyards, wine cellar lanes, and tasting events, is a frequent destination for many wine lovers. Furthermore, Langenlois is popular with tourists, who can often be seen walking alongside the river Kamp.

In Langenlois, the commercial and vocational schools offered a 2-year education, with no school leaving exams. Many of the pupils finishing this school didn't pursue any higher education. In order to pursue university studies after completion, one had the choice to attend other Franciscans schools, in the towns of Zwettl or Amstetten. Nowadays, the focus of the school in Langenlois has shifted to social care, and its new name *Fachschule für Sozialberufe* (Vocational/Secondary school for social professions) stresses this change.

Thinking back on the school curriculum and the variety of subjects makes me smile. We learnt German, English, informatics, economics, and typewriting (on rather old-fashioned typewriters) and even sewing, cooking, nutrition, baking, table decoration, and food serving. There were moments of excitement and creativity, alongside moments of grumpiness, especially when we had to learn how to use a rag. Whether we were being shown how to clean with the rag, or how to squeeze the dirty water from it, you would often hear students complaining about this particular task. I was interested in everything creative, for example sawing, and the production of handmade stuffed toys, batik scarves, and jewellery.

At this time, I was at an early stage in my eating disorder, and therefore preferred not to focus on food. Yet still, cooking and baking were a key part of the curriculum, so I had to deal with them. The hours spent in these lessons felt like torture, but I didn't want anyone to find out. It was all made much harder by the fact that we were obliged to taste and eat everything that we had prepared ourselves.

In truth, my inner self started to suffer long before my stay in Langenlois. The goodness of the nuns, my teachers, and the friends I made, unfortunately couldn't prevent my emotional breakdown. I suffered because I couldn't change my parents' relationship. They were so unhappy, and hurting each other. During my stay in Langenlois, there was one situation I will never forget. My parents came for a visit, and while my mother discussed organisational matters with the Franciscan Sisters and other mothers, my father and I sat on a bench outside the building. He cried, and told me that he didn't know what to do – their marriage was full of struggles. He felt so exhausted. A life spent under the rule of the totalitarian regime, living in poverty, scarcity, and fear, had taken its toll on their relationship. As someone who had been hypersensitive since my early childhood, I was but a flower on a thin stem, that a strong wind could break. And soon, the wind came.

The First Eight

In Langenlois, the RC Sisters didn't have it easy. We were teenagers, filled with energy, and it's fair to say the Sisters had their hands full. With this in mind, it was important to organise programmes which would keep us busy. To add to the level of responsibility, some girls (including me) actually boarded at the school, whereas others travelled from neighbouring villages in order to attend classes. So, even when they weren't teaching, the Sisters were taking care of pupils, and making sure we stayed out of mischief.

For all of us Slovak pupils, the first year at the school was very challenging. We didn't speak good German, and therefore our teacher had to give us additional lessons after school. Learning German felt like paradise on earth. My passion for foreign languages grew each day. At the beginning, our grades were average, but gradually the excellence of the eight Slovak girls made the Franciscans very proud. In the second year, we didn't only finish with the best grades, but we also improved the overall grade average of the entire class. The Austrian pupils admired our intelligence and hard work. The first weeks in Langenlois were full of verbal misunderstandings and faux pas, but we didn't give up. We communicated not only in school with our classmates, but also in our bedrooms. The nuns were clever to mix Slovaks with Austrians, so we basically had no choice but to speak with each other. We liked the Austrian girls, since they showed a genuine interest in our culture. Together, we listened to the famous Slovak pop band, *Elán*, and shared our sweets. Most of the bedrooms had four beds. About twenty five girls used the bathroom and toilets, situated in the hallway. We all had a schedule to follow. Breakfast, morning classes, lunch, afternoon classes, late afternoon learning with leisure activities, dinner – everything was scheduled. After the evening hygiene, we were asked to stay in our rooms and rest. In the evening, after a certain hour, the Sisters watched the corridor for any "suspicious" movements.

The more you forbid something, the more appealing it is. We cleverly sneaked from room to room. We spent many hours talking about music, boys, boy bands, and other less attractive topics with our friends. Challenged by the darkness, we sat in a circle in the centre of the room or on beds, and ate sweets. Apart from small pocket lamps, we couldn't use any other source of light, as the upper part of each bedroom door was made of glass. We tried to organise ourselves to avoid having too many people in one room. Once we heard steps in the hallway, we jumped into beds and covered ourselves with duvets. Two people per bed was fine, more than two proved to be rather difficult.

What we didn't realise, was that the Franciscan Sisters had concerns regarding our safety. Young, naïve Slovak girls in their early teens could become an easy target for perverts or xenophobes. There were set times during the week where we could walk outside, in groups, usually in the afternoon. The Sisters preferred that we stayed within the premises to learn, play games, or help a bit with gardening. During the time spent in town we regularly checked our wrist watches, in order to avoid coming back late. According to rumours, the area around the picturesque town of Langenlois didn't offer foreigners a safe environment. People claimed that in the 1990s, neo-Nazis used to have *Kameradschaften* gatherings, and their *Wehrsportgruppen* clubs, which were basically "military training sessions", in that particular area. One can only imagine the worries and concerns of the Franciscan Sisters we were entrusted to by our parents.

There are so many stereotypes regarding Roman Catholic boarding schools for girls. Those who assumed that boys secretly entered the premises, and that the girls smuggled in alcohol, would be disappointed. Believe it or not, we didn't consider the school a prison. All eight of us Slovak girls had a good time playing badminton and ball games outside in the yard, with Ludo and other games inside. On weekends, we also watched videos. I think I saw Top Gun and Dirty Dancing over thirty times. I used to know many of the dialogues between Baby and Johnny off by heart. I also tried to copy their dance moves, learning parts of their very exciting choreographies. Even at that early stage in my life, dancing had become a real passion of mine.

Today, when I close my eyes, I can still see the Franciscan premises of Langenlois in front of me; the ground floor with the kindergarten that was separated from the other premises and the hallways with a little fountain. Outside, one could see trees, a garden, a playground for children, and an area for ball games. I would say that the buildings, their interior, and the yard, were both modern and colourful.

The Franciscan Sisters made sure we were healthy and that we had all we needed. We were treated well. The Sisters knew who we were – children from Czechoslovakia, most of whom had experienced poverty, whose Christian families had suffered under a totalitarian regime. It is interesting how people who've experienced poverty react differently when they are suddenly surrounded by material goods and many choices. Some approach the goods in a careful and modest way, enjoying them bit by bit. Others aim to have as many things as possible, in a short period of time. I was usually the latter. When we sewed a blouse, I wanted to have more than one. When we produced handmade jewellery or scarves, one piece of each wasn't enough. Producing handmade stuffed toys meant that my toy had to be as big as possible. Looking at so many beautiful things, I wanted them all. In the Roman Catholic boarding school, we learned and lived in a protected environment, where many choices were made for us. Later in my life, I realised that the pursuit of modesty in modern society, where we face so many tempting choices, can be quite challenging.

In Langenlois, to this day we are known as "The first eight", since we were the first eight Slovak girls to complete secondary school there. Looking back, I treasure this period in my life, and it was a time of fond memories.

Guilty Pleasures

In Czechoslovakia, teens and adults didn't know much about pornography or drugs. Society didn't have to deal with such issues like it does today. Drugs and pornography were perceived as the illnesses of the West.

There was something elegant about watching television in the 1980s. Everyone enjoyed being greeted by attractive TV presenters with pleasant voices, informing us about the programmes to follow. The female presenters had what you would today describe as "star-status"; people admired them and were curious about their lives.

I remember the time when commercials didn't cut films into pieces. Today, films are interrupted by TV spots far too often; we even have problems remembering the storylines. Thousands of commercial images try to tell us what goods and services we need in order to feel complete. Young women dressed in tight clothes are looking at the camera, directly into our eyes, and claiming, 'If you want to have an attractive body, eat this yogurt' or 'If you want to have beautiful hair, use this conditioner.' Sex sells. Marketers know exactly how to (mis)use sexually appealing images to help sell products and services. During my childhood, society was not oversexualised like it is today.

Only once during my childhood did I see pornographic pictures. It happened when my family and I visited friends that we used to buy pigs from. The adults talked and drank inside the house, while we children played in the yard. We knew that for safety reasons we were not allowed to enter the garage, which served as a workroom, nor the area where all the animals had their stalls. We were asked to play on the grass area only. Of course, the moment we saw an opportunity to enter the garage, we did. We wanted to see all the equipment and machines, we knew they had bikes and bicycles. To be honest, I don't remember the bike, but I do remember the posters with naked women on the walls. Standing there, quite surprised, I couldn't believe what I was looking at. Until that day, the only naked woman I had seen was my mother. I was not only surprised at the different body shapes and private parts, but also about the fact that women posed naked. My sister and I didn't spend much time in that garage, as the adults came to find us within minutes – they'd sensed that there might be something wrong, as we were oddly silent. To our surprise, they didn't shout at us – but quickly led us away from the garage.

Although my parents were negative about extramarital sex, they willingly answered our questions regarding the menstrual cycle, human anatomy, voice breaking, sexual intercourse, pregnancy, and childbirth. We didn't speak about contraception, as our parents didn't know much about pills or condoms. On one occasion, Mama laughingly said, 'When I saw a condom for the first time, I thought it was a single-pack of little soap.'

For the most part, I think that associating "sex" with "sin" is quite damaging. Of course, there are lots of exceptions to the rule (rape, for example), but growing up as a Catholic resulted in lots of confusion. Roman Catholics have so many rules to follow, and so many bans and commands. My sister and I were quite fortunate that our parents at least answered our questions regarding human sexuality. Many Christians avoided addressing this topic altogether, since, in their opinion, intimacy as a part of marital life should have been discovered by the married couple. The most absurd statement I heard as a teenager was that married couples should only have sexual intercourse for the sole purpose of having children.

During the two years spent in Langenlois, I realised how different views on sexuality can be. In Austria, as well as in other countries "of the West", young people were reading the magazine *Bravo*, where Dr. Sommer educated them on love, sex, and tenderness. My classmates in Langenlois read the magazine regularly. Out of curiosity, I borrowed it once. I was fourteen years old, and the naked bodies and information on sex positions were too graphic. References to STDs terrified me. Regarding intimacy, I felt that the girls' world and the boys' world were very different. We Slovak girls talked about dating, walking down the streets with a boy, holding hands, and the first kiss. We had many romantic fantasies, but sex just wasn't really a topic (yet).

I grew up with the conviction that being a virgin was a privilege. Virginity was a gift; once I met my life partner and we married, I would experience something special with him. The truth is, during my studies in Vienna, I didn't follow what I was taught. I wanted to experience intimacy sooner than marriage, but that doesn't mean I didn't have romantic fantasies and expectations for my first time. Manuel, my Austrian colleague at the university, attended Russian seminars with me. I was impressed when Austrians managed to complete Russian studies, since it is a rather difficult language for them. I saw several Austrian students give up after only a couple of hours. I remember the Russian seminars were popular amongst Slavic students, as it wasn't a difficult language for them to learn. Austrians studying at the Business University in Vienna however, preferred seminars in Spanish or French, since those were the languages they had started to learn during secondary school.

Manuel struggled initially with learning Russian, but he attended the seminar regularly. We sat next to each other, and I tried to look at him without him noticing. A friendly face, shoulder length dark, curly hair, athletic figure – from the very first lesson I already felt attracted to him. We talked a lot, sometimes over a coffee after our seminar. With the passing of time, we started to date, and I learnt that he was an experienced man who had already been in a two-year relationship. I didn't say much about my past, so he mistakenly thought I was experienced too. I acted self-confident, and wasn't completely honest, as I tended to hide my insecurities.

We visited each other in dormitories, and for a longer period of time we engaged in kissing only. Manuel couldn't hide his surprise after I told him that I was a virgin. He acted disappointed, and I wasn't sure whether to stay or go. Well, I stayed. I didn't enjoy my first sexual experience with a man that much. It hurt, and I was glad when it ended. After I started to put on my clothes, Manuel asked me why I wasn't staying for the night. I found an excuse and walked six bus stops back to where I was accommodated. All my romantic notions melted away. The lower part of my body hurt. Disappointment and negative thoughts started to sneak into my soul.

Today, I see my reaction to my first intimacy with a man as the beginning of a strange behavioural pattern. It's something I am not proud of. Men would first make an impression on me with their appearance, behaviour, opinions, and humour. We started to date, and gradually became intimate. However, I couldn't truly enjoy my sexuality, as after every intimate experience, I knew I would have to speak about it during my confession at the church. As intimacy often made me feel anxious, I preferred to stay alone for months without any intimate relationship. I gradually realised that there was something wrong, after the number of partners I'd left began to increase. I was running away; fleeing from situations that I struggled to cope with.

I often think about all the rules I follow as a member of the Church. Do the rules guide me, or do they paralyse me? There is something fundamentally wrong, when sexuality is accompanied by shame and guilt, rather than feeling God-given and beautiful. Maybe in shifting the focus from sins and sin management, to God's Grace, we can help to see ourselves differently.

Lying in My Bed

Dreams can be beautiful, fascinating, and sometimes unexpectedly hellish.

My bed is a magical place, and I am grateful that most of my dreams are pleasant and peaceful. I remember many of them. I often dream about water, as does my father, and his father before him. In those dreams, I am usually swimming in a lake or sea, but sometimes I am just standing on the seashore, watching the shimmering water. In my dreams, I am often able to perform activities that I could never have performed in reality, such as swimming long distances. If dreams are, to a certain extent, an indicator of what I am capable of, then my potential is huge indeed. I am convinced that we are all capable of great accomplishments, and of participating in exciting activities, as we all have the capacity to learn.

Once, I dreamed that I lived in a forest, alone in my own house, situated next to a river. I was able to repair everything in and around the house. I also chopped the wood I collected and created fires to keep myself warm. What was amazing about this particular dream is the fact that I had knowledge about the medical use of different herbs. I knew when and where to collect them, as well as how to process them. This knowledge enabled me to aid people knocking at my door, asking for help.

I do wonder why I often dream of water, but of course there is no clear answer. I think of water as a symbol of life, purity, and freedom. Water represents the limitlessness of the spirit. For me, seas and lakes are places filled with tranquillity, beauty, and retreat. They also symbolise powerful forces of nature that we can't control. It's fascinating what a dreamer's mind experiences, what is known and seen, and what is hidden. Sometimes I wake up and think of the place I dreamt of. Have I ever really been there? Will I go there in future?

Almost every person goes through days of sleeplessness from time to time. Being human means being capable of worrying about the future and rehashing the past. Some people can't sleep one day, others struggle to sleep for more than a few hours. Insomnia is marked by difficulty falling asleep or staying asleep, or both.

Lying in My Bed

My bed is magical, but it is also my own personal hell.

During sleepless nights, my heart races. I feel dizzy, and lie there sweating and trembling. It's a frightening experience. My bed turns into a battleground, where I stare for hours at the ceiling, and my inner world begins to fill with bad memories and pain. During the day, I am working. I am busy with meeting people and completing my projects. When the night comes, there is no way to escape from my thoughts.

In order to combat this, I have created my own pre-sleep routine, which helps me to relax. It consists of listening to calming music, taking a bath, and repeating affirmations and prayers. In the past, I have also taken medication – but of course this is far from ideal.

Tonight, laying in my bed, I hope to drift off and dream about the beauty of nature. A good night's sleep is one of the secrets to a successful life. Waking up energised, on a regular basis, contributes to a healthier mind and well-being.

It's Not About Obesity,
It's About Love

Who am I? For years I struggled with identity. I knew neither who I was, nor what I really wanted to do in my life. I felt that I had no control, that there was a strict set of rules to follow without much joy and encouragement.

Problems with my weight started very early. As a nine-year-old, I often ate simply for warmth and comfort. I ate mainly bread and butter. Sometimes, between meals, I took food from a nice wooden cupboard – called the "bar" – which was situated in our living room. Many Slovak households had such cupboards, filled with alcohol, nuts, and sweets that they would offer to their guests. My sister would sometimes take things from the bar too, and therefore our parents did not know who ate what. I began to grow bigger and bigger, but I only became really overweight during one particular summer with my grandparents.

Since both our parents worked full-time, and had no money for a nanny, our paternal grandparents often took care of me and my sister during the summer months. We went for many town walks, and were given money for the amusement park, where we rode on the carousels until we felt sick. We travelled to many different cities, enjoyed sightseeing, and went to the zoo. Our grandpa even repaired two old bicycles, so that we could enjoy our adventures cycling around the town. They hugged and kissed us. We felt so pampered. Nobody stopped me from eating, and when I asked for more, I was given more. When they came to pick us up at the end of the summer, my parents were truly shocked with my weight. I cannot say that it was my grandparents' fault for this – they meant well, and all they wanted was for my sister and I to have all we needed.

My weight was also an issue at school. The behaviour of some of my classmates changed abruptly. I was not as popular as before. Certain smiles seemed to be rather fake, even taunting. To be judged upon appearance was something previously unknown to me. Children can be so cruel. All of a sudden, I didn't have as many friends as before. Even my second childhood sweetheart, Roman, stopped talking to me. He would previously shyly smile at me, and give me colourful drawings – that was enough for me to call him my boyfriend. I did however have two female friends, both called Andrea, who were nice to me and didn't mind that I had physically changed.

Life is a rollercoaster of emotions. I did not feel good at school, nor at home. I was depressed and lonely. Once a child who couldn't stop eating, I gradually became a child that refused to eat. I was twelve years old, and my mental health had already started to deteriorate. The truth is, words can be like swords. They cause wounds that take a long time to heal. It's difficult to forget phrases like, 'You're always so clumsy.' 'Since you aren´t very smart, it is good that you are a hard-worker.' 'You are incapable of remembering some simple dates related to WWII? You have to try harder!' 'You must eat everything that is given to you!' Adults often don´t nurture self-confidence in children, and they don't realise that the words they use can have a lasting impact on impressionable young ones.

I wanted a better life, but I didn't know how to achieve it. If there was one thing that nobody else had control over, I thought, it was my body. I started to believe that if I improved the way I looked, I would be seen, noticed by others. In order to become popular and loved, I decided to remodel myself, and "make myself more likeable". Eating only small portions, and taking a ridiculously long amount of time to eat, helped me to lose weight. I started making myself sick, but later I turned to excessive exercising, to try and burn as many calories as possible. After not having my period for months, I knew that I wasn't giving my body the nutrients it needed. My body was changing, as was my personality. I became tired and irritable, with neither the energy nor patience to listen to conversations. I started to really suffer, but had no idea that my condition had a name. Anorexia Nervosa is a serious mental health condition. It's not a diet gone wrong. The sufferer has a distorted image of themselves. They can't cope with difficult issues in their lives. Anorexia, as well as bulimia (with episodes of binge eating as well as self-induced vomiting), are serious diseases which, left untreated, can lead to death. One starves her or himself to death. On my worst days, I was only 42 kg – considering my height of 167 cm, I looked very thin and fragile.

Anorexia comes with self-deceiving and deceiving others. I told my parents I ate at school, or asked if I could eat in my room as I had to study. Instead of eating the food in my room, I put it into a plastic bag and hid it. Excessive exercising with occasional self-induced vomiting led to exhaustion. At school I could not focus properly and I had to constantly force myself to learn in class and communicate with my sister and friends. Everything was such a burden. I cried a lot, in solitude and silence. Every day I became more and more depressed. My parents began to worry, as I became increasingly thinner and quieter. After my mother caught me vomiting in the toilet, she no longer believed that my stomach was irritated or that I had a food allergy. My mother didn't know much about eating disorders (none of us did), but her instincts were really good. She confronted me and I told her everything, realising I couldn´t hide it any longer.

Although I was angry with what I perceived as a loss of control, at the same time I felt relieved, as I was exhausted from all the secret rituals. My mother took all the necessary steps to ensure I was admitted to the hospital for treatment. Psychiatrists prescribed anti-depressants and sleeping pills. Psychologists showed me papers with some blobs on them and I had to say what I saw. I know they tried to create something like a "personal and sickness profile", but I felt like a guinea pig most of the time. The doctors did not really speak with me to find out how I felt, as there was more focus on pills than counselling.

There was, however, one opportunity I didn't want to miss. I was offered art therapy, and it felt as if somebody was whispering, 'Here is a balm for your suffering body and tormented soul.' I remember the day I entered the room with all the beautiful materials, shiny colours, and tools. Still at the hospital, I decided to begin with handmade jewellery production. I kept drafting and producing earrings, bracelets, and necklaces for many years after the completion of the art therapy. Members of my family and friends received jewellery as a gift, and were happy about it, since I never produced the same piece twice. I loved to touch and process various materials like wool, shells, metal, wood, and glass.

The weeks I spent in the hospital were scary and humiliating. I hated the side effects of the pills I was taking. The hospital staff had eyes everywhere. I felt lonely until I met Magda, a young girl who had suffered a lot, and often seemed confused. She liked me and shared some of her problems and therapy information with me. I heard for the first time about Electroconvulsive Therapy, and I was stunned. I would never allow anyone to use an electric current on me! In spite of all her pain, Magda somehow managed to talk to me, and we became friends. During the time I spent in hospital, I did not want to see any friends or classmates, and it was painful to see a priest too – who had been sent by my parents. I blamed God for many things. I thought that he was not helping me, and that he was being cruel. I wasn't sure if God is a loving father or a sadist, who enjoys playing strange games with us. Magda was very religious. She didn't seek my company just to speak, but also so that we could pray together. Sometimes I prayed grudgingly, but I did not want to say no to Magda, who always asked me to accompany her. It was surprising to me how she could be so close to God. She spoke so lovingly about Him. My friendship with Magda lasted several months. For many years afterwards, I didn't know anything about her life, until she contacted me through a social network. Today, Magda is married and has a baby – words and pictures indicate that she is happy.

Despite the terrible situation in which I found myself, I didn't lose hope. I hoped that things would improve, that I would become better. However, becoming healthy again was difficult. Unlike a person who is addicted to a substance and will abstain from it, a person with an eating disorder must eat every day. I started to eat regular portions at least three times per day. I knew that if I didn't eat, I would die. People who think that refusing to eat is all about food, vanity, and weight are very wrong. It's important to read about eating disorders and ask sufferers, if you want to understand the complexity of such disorders. A sufferer needs to do more than "just eat". During my stay in the hospital, I realised that I needed to start a journey towards self-acceptance. I focused on changing the negative thought patterns which caused the eating disorder in the first place. Since counselling therapy wasn't as common as it is today, I tried to find books about psychology. Reading *You Can Heal Your Life* by Louise L. Hay contributed to changing my thoughts. Repeating chosen affirmations helped me to replace negative thoughts with positive ones. By concentrating on my breathing during the autogenic training, I started to relax.

As I got stronger, I started to understand that every person is a complex mix of experiences and emotions. Once I'd found a way to clearly identify the sorrow and grief, I decided to look at my childhood and family situation in a rational way. The food obsession drowned out so many emotions. Most people are unaware of the impact of a traumatic childhood, or the negative results of conflict during childhood. Still a teenager, I knew that I wouldn't stay with my family forever. One day, I would choose my own way to live. I disagreed with the authoritarian behaviour of my parents, and therefore I decided to speak confidentially with some family members to understand it better.

Many adults use the parenting style they've experienced during their childhood. My mother and father cared for me and my sister, they provided us with material goods and they always tried to teach us new things. However, since they both experienced physical punishment during their childhood, I assume that they thought certain "punishments" were a normal part of bringing up children. Change in behaviour is only possible if the parents consciously decide against something they went through when they were little. My sister, for example, decided a long time ago to never physically punish her children.

Strict parenting becomes even more dangerous when the strict set of rules isn't balanced out with open communication, enabling the child to understand why it is important to follow the rules. Speaking about the rules can also help to uncover those which are having a negative impact on a child's self-esteem. I will never understand why my parents were disappointed because I received the second-best grade at school. Punishing me for a positive, yet not perfect grade, made me think I was not good enough.

The truth is, I am good enough. I have many talents. Not only did I recover from an eating disorder, but I also discovered my creative potential.

Today, reading in the newspaper about obese children and how we need to fight obesity with physical activity and healthy food throws me back in time, and I think about the suffering children, longing for love and closeness. Believe me, physical activity and healthy food isn't enough to make a child happy. Children need something more permanent. They need loving care and affection, to be better equipped for the life ahead of them.

Vienna

During my business studies in Vienna, I lived with the Roman Catholic Sisters – the Sisters of the Divine Saviour (*Schwestern vom Göttlichen Erlöser* in German). The Sisters helped me with accommodation, and in exchange, we agreed that I would assist them when necessary. The RC Sisters live under vows of chastity, voluntary poverty, religious obedience, and fraternal community. Their values and sense of community have always fascinated me. Most of the time I call nuns "my sisters", because this is what I am used to. There is a lot of respect. For me, it's difficult to understand why people would leave mainstream society, and enter a convent. Pursuing a life of prayer and silent contemplation is so different to the norm, and the courage and dedication of the nuns is a source of endless interest to me.

The founder of the Sisters of the Divine Saviour was Elisabeth Eppinger, with her religious name Mother Alphonse Marie. The Sisters told me that Elisabeth was born in Niederbronn-les-Bains in Alsace, France. From a very early stage in her life, she felt that she wanted to dedicate herself to helping people in mental and physical distress. Many women joined her, and to this day, women still join the Sisters of the Divine Savour. I have met many nuns from Austria, Germany, France, Slovakia, and India. In Vienna, the Sisters devote their time and energy to educating young people, caring for the sick and elderly, helping the homeless, and praying for and with people during prayer gatherings.

The building complex where I lived in Vienna was situated on three adjacent streets. Within the complex, one could find various schools, including a boarding school for girls, a nursery, a church, a convent, and a small hotel for guests participating in religious gatherings. The spacious yard and playground made the entire area look even bigger. The rooms for girls who attended the boarding school were located above the nursery, throughout the fifth and sixth floor. A group of vulnerable girls who needed special care, due to their family situations and disorders, were accommodated on the fourth floor. The girls were taken care of by nuns, as well as experienced professionals. Somebody very close to my heart was Sister Judith.

My room was situated in the corner of the sixth floor, close to the phone that we all had access to. There was a direct line which was installed in the foyer area, on all floors next to the lift. I perceived this as being more than a little annoying, as it kept ringing, and none of the calls were for me. I often ran out of my room, towards the hallway phone, only to hear a cleaning lady calling to ask to speak to another cleaning lady. The hallway phones didn't serve for just internal communication. Families and friends of the schoolgirls called regularly. When I picked up the phone to say, 'Good afternoon, boarding school, Eva speaking' (*Grüß Gott, Internat, Eva*) they automatically assumed I was a nun, and addressed me as 'Sister Eva'. It was quite funny at first, but after having to explain so often that I wasn't a nun, I eventually gave up and accepted being addressed as Sister Eva. After I learnt who wanted to speak to whom, I had to walk down the corridor to knock on their door. Needless to say, it was rather tiresome to do this several times per day.

In Austria, I never got used to the fact that children attended classes on Saturdays. Growing up, we never went to school on weekends. I felt pity for the children whose weekends were filled with studying instead of fun. Since their families lived far away from Vienna, the girls only travelled home for the weekends. Fortunately, nobody expected them to travel often, so they continued boarding school during the week. On Saturday, after the morning classes, they travelled home for the weekend.

At the school, I had various tasks every week. I helped out in the office on the ground floor and took care of the front door. The girls were only allowed to leave the premises of the boarding school during certain hours. I opened the doors for the girls after they rang a buzzer, and I answered the phone to welcome visitors. When it was needed, I also assisted in the small hotel, situated on the street adjacent to the boarding school. The hotel played an important role in welcoming guests, who were visiting Vienna to take part in various religious activities.

During the many years I spent in Vienna, I tried so hard to find a way to make a living. I wanted to be a good person; I tried to obey, study, and work. But I was disoriented. I worked for four years as a babysitter to start earning a small amount of money. It was difficult to find a job in Vienna, since in the '90s the Slovak Republic wasn't one of the EU member states, and the EU labour market wasn't fully open to Slovaks. My parents largely financed my studies, and I felt ashamed of that. Despite all my efforts, I studied slowly, and had to repeat some exams two or three times. I struggled mainly with any subjects I didn't have a passion for.

At that time in my life, I often did what my parents wanted me to. My sister didn't want to study, and because of that she faced problems at home. Our parents were repeatedly telling her that she was wasting her talents. She persisted, and got married at twenty – to a man my parents were sceptical about. Although I didn't have the ambition to study, I studied nonetheless, and felt drained. Years passed by, and it seemed like I would never finish.

Despite some difficulties, I admit that I enjoyed reading the theological and philosophical books that I found on the Sisters' shelves, rather than books about cost calculation and statistics. What really surprised me was the fact that I am interested in so many different fields – like law, theology, geography, poetry, and the arts. I didn't like the pressure to choose one field and one field only. I was an adult who didn't have one true calling, and it stressed me enormously. Was I a failure? My parents and teachers expected me to know what I wanted to do with my life from the age of seven years old. In my twenties I didn't know what I know today – I was a multipotentialite.

A Young Romanian Man

In Vienna, the Roman Catholic Sisters helped many homeless and marginalised people. I was sometimes unexpectedly involved in their social and charitable activities. One afternoon, during the working week, a nun I didn't know very well called and asked me for help.

I said yes, of course, and made my way to the area between the hotel and church on the adjacent street. There were so many lifts, corridors, and cellar rooms in that building complex – one could easily have gotten lost in the labyrinth. As soon as I arrived at the agreed spot, I noticed a young man standing next to the sister, who explained that he was Romanian and couldn't speak German. She wanted to find out if he spoke a common language to me. Looking at the young man, my first impressions were of a smelly, sad-faced individual, with dirty clothes. After a brief moment, I realised I shouldn't be paying attention to such things, and instead focused on giving him the help he needed. I looked at him directly, with a friendly face, and greeted him in English. My first attempt failed, as he reacted in Romanian. I next thought to try Russian. To my surprise, the man started to reply in distinctly broken Russian. Excellent! The man was named Andrei. He was in his early twenties, and had decided to improve his life by travelling to Austria and looking for a job there. After spending three weeks in Austria, he ran out of money and slept on the streets of Vienna. At Westbahnhof station, somebody told him that there were nuns in the Kaiserstraße, and that he should ask for help there.

I communicated everything he said to the sister, and she asked for his ID. He said his ID was stolen; I assumed he was simply scared that we would report him to the police. Together with the sister, we decided not to analyse if he was lying or not, and we instead tried helping him. Andrei said that he needed to take a shower, eat something, sleep somewhere, and find a way to receive money from his family via Western Union – so he could travel to Germany where his friends lived. The Sister asked me to translate her response: 'You can take a shower here, we will give you food, wash your clothes, and Eva will help you find accommodation in a shelter. We'll also help to contact your family about the transfer of money.'

We agreed to meet again in two hours, and I went back to my room. Shortly after, the hallway phone rang. It was the same sister, asking me to return as soon as I could. I dashed out to meet her. She explained that while Andrei was taking a shower, she'd tried to wash his clothes, but realised that his shirt, trousers, and underwear weren't in a good condition. As the Sisters often received clothing donations, she was able to find an extra shirt and trousers for him. After she told me why I had to return earlier than agreed, my jaw dropped. She gave me 5 euros and said to quickly buy two or three pieces of male underwear at Mariahilfer Straße, a well-known Vienna shopping street, situated two minutes from the convent. I couldn't hide my astonishment, so she added, 'I am sure you understand that I cannot really go and buy him underwear.' Looking at her friendly face and her head covered in coif and veil, I knew I was going to have to buy male underwear for the first time – for a man I didn't even know. I smiled slightly at the idea of the sister, dressed in her habit, buying male underwear, and the face of the shop assistant – priceless.

After I bought the necessary boxers, in two different sizes, and Andrei finished cleaning himself up, we decided to look for accommodation. Evening was approaching, and we therefore walked quickly towards "the Gruft", a homeless shelter on the Mariahilfer Straße. The Gruft was situated directly below the Church of Mariahilf, and it was run by Caritas, a charitable organisation that is active in many countries across the world.

In the Gruft, people sought shelter, food, and information related to social services. As soon as we entered, Andrei told me that he was not used to such places. I asked him what he meant, and he explained that he'd never slept in a shelter, and that he was scared. He couldn't stay in a smelly room, filled with men lying on mattresses and blankets, worrying about somebody stealing his remaining belongings or causing him harm. I assured him that the room was supervised, but Andrei ran out of the church building, and I followed after him. Outside the building, he said he would rather sleep on the street. I faced a dilemma, since I didn't want to leave him like that. We returned back to Kaiserstraße to speak to the Sister again. Since there was no time to look for alternative accommodation, the Sister said she was going to ask if he could stay in a room within the building. The Sisters of the Divine Saviour had guest rooms, but they were usually reserved for clergy and laypeople joining Christian events. She told me that the other reason why she was a bit worried was in regards to safety, as Andrei was a stranger. She left to discuss it with the other Sisters, and I was left waiting with Andrei for the final decision. Eventually, he was given a room to rest, and we agreed to resolve the Western Union issue the following day.

Early the next morning, I picked up Andrei, and we went to the Westbahnhof station. The night was quiet, with no problems. The Sisters told me that he was a polite, shy boy – thankful for everything he received. When we arrived at the train station, I gave Andrei some coins and he called his family in Romania. We then went to a Western Union store, and I filled in a form with my details and provided my proof of ID. It didn't take long for Andrei to receive a modest sum of money from his family. He thanked me for everything, and then left. I have never seen or heard from him again.

I hope that Andrei is doing well. Looking back at the time spent in Vienna with the Roman Catholic Sisters makes me realise that I have been surrounded by clergy members throughout my life. They helped me with education, work, and strengthened my social awareness. I'm thankful for that, and it has made me a more empathetic and compassionate person.

Pre-Christmas Party for Homeless

In Vienna, I attended many Christian events and prayer meetings, and participated in social projects. Some of my experiences touched my soul. The first time I joined an event designed to help the homeless, I was rather nervous. It was a pre-Christmas dinner, where I would be serving food and talking to the guests. When one of the nuns approached me to enquire about the event and the serving help they needed, I instantly said yes.

The nun informed me that the event was going to take place on the 22nd of December, in a larger room on the ground floor, next to the convent. She briefly explained the programme, who was expected to attend, and what time the dinner would be served. I understood there would be nuns, a priest, social workers, and a policeman in attendance. She further explained that up to fifty people were going to enter the room from the street – homeless men and women. We would be serving vegetable soup with bread, and non-alcoholic drinks like tea and lemonade. Subsequently, we would form small groups at the tables, to engage in conversation and encouragement. Before leaving, those in need would be given clothes, and everyone would receive a package containing food. She told me that food wasn't the only area of help we'd provide. The Sisters collected clothes from people who brought them to the church to give to those in need, and they even knitted some of the caps and gloves themselves.

The event itself was peaceful and pleasant. I did my best to smile, although I was filled with sadness and compassion looking at the homeless women. Until that day, I hadn't seen women living on the streets of Bratislava or Vienna. I came to understand that suffering doesn't discriminate; men and women of all ages and backgrounds can be affected. At the beginning of the evening, everyone was greeted and seated at the wooden tables. Once the official welcome speech and short prayer ended, we started serving dinner. Some people wanted more of the bread or vegetable soup that the nuns had prepared for them, and therefore three young girls, including myself, were required to assist. We later brought everyone a non-alcoholic drink. The atmosphere was calm, one could even hear the clinking of spoons.

As often happens in life, peaceful moments don't last long. Our evening was abruptly interrupted by a burning Christmas tree. One of the beeswax candles placed on a holder had "lost its balance", and the tree caught fire. Somebody standing close to the tree screamed out, and to my surprise, several people with fast reflexes poured their lemonade on it to extinguish the fire – which worked surprisingly well.

I served food and drink, and hardly took a break. I wanted it to be a nice, even memorable evening for everyone. The majority of the guests at the tables were Austrians, but some were Slavic and Romanian as well. Many people travel to foreign countries with the aim of improving their lives, but not everyone succeeds. Arriving in a foreign country, not speaking the language, and having difficulty learning it, leads people into bad situations and having heavy dependency on others.

Dinner was followed by a short prayer. The police officer said goodbye, but at the door, turned and stressed, 'I hope I won't be needed.' One of the guests asked me which country I was from, and if my intention was to become a nun. I told him that I am from Slovakia. His reaction surprised me a bit, since he spoke about Czechoslovakia and about the peaceful split of the two nations – Slovaks and Czechs. He told me about his life, his biology studies, and his marriage. He said, 'You know, my wife and I used to quarrel often, I felt so exhausted. I worked a lot and alcohol helped me escape many problems. I thought it did. But one day she left me and took the kids with her. The divorce was painful. I hardly ever see the children. With the passing of time, I couldn't stand the lonely evenings in the flat. I drank more. Lost my job and then the flat too. Then I ended up on the street and drank even more alcohol.' We sat there, silently, side by side. I did not know what to say. I had no intension of impressing him with my "words of wisdom", as it wasn't the right time to speak. He understood the expression on my face. Words were not necessary.

This event had a strong impact on me. The thought of serving those who usually aren't being served, made me joyful. By the end of the evening, I felt like I had experienced something special, and that I grew as a person because of it.

Judith

'Judith, please tell me a bit about the Vienna Secession.'
'Ok, let's go into my room.'

We entered a modestly furnished room with only a minimal interior – a wardrobe, a bed, a table with two chairs, and a sink. Sister Judith's room was as modest as her. But perhaps, this should have not been so unusual. After all, she was a Roman Catholic nun of the Order of the Sisters of the Divine Saviour.

We sat down, and Judith decided to create a nice atmosphere by turning on a small table lamp, and switching off the main light. While she was lighting a candle on the table, she started to speak about art. A passionate artist, Judith's paintings and her way of communicating messages of spirituality, beauty, and God's love, are unique. Judith is an excellent communicator, a great speaker who knew when to say the right words and when to listen. Most of the people who have had the privilege of meeting Judith never forget her intelligence, friendliness, humour, and empathy.

Clerics are often perceived as being disconnected from everyday reality, not knowing much about the problems that other people face. Many times throughout my life, I've heard people claim that the clergy's rigour and sense of superiority are stronger than their love and compassion. Looking at Sister Judith, I see how dangerous such generalising statements can be. In my opinion, those who want to see the bad in people, see only the bad. For the one who focuses mainly on mistakes, imperfections, and flaws, the beauty in life seems like a distant, unknown concept. Clerics are people, and people make mistakes. Whoever expects the Church, consisting of people, to be perfect, will end up waiting forever. The Church is like a sister to me. I care about her, while being aware of her difficulties. In Judith I also see a sister, as she has had a massive influence on my life. I do not think she even realises it. Her friendly personality and the many discussions we had resonate with me to this day. Most of all, I remember her sisterly love. I am thankful for her reactions when I shared my struggles with her. She always listened and tried to understand what I was going through. Judith never judged me, and always showed me her emotions. I will never forget her warm hugs. Today, since we live in two different countries, we communicate mostly online.

Judith's beauty can be seen in her paintings too. *Samenkorn* (The Seed) is a stunning painting, showing all the phases of life together – the seed put in the soil, the plant growing from it, the tree bearing the fruit – all borne by the Earth. Christians know the parable of the mustard seed well. The seemingly insignificant mustard seed initially looks so small next to a sunflower or flax seed. Although little, it has tremendous hidden potential – it bides its time, becomes stronger, and grows until it transforms into a massive bush. The mustard seed in the parable probably emphasises the degree of faith in God, and the power of small beginnings turning into enormous growth.

When I think of Judith's painting, I tend to look at my own life, with all its changes. I believe that even the smallest of actions, when combined with continuous effort, can lead to big results. Everything has a beginning. No matter how small or humble our own beginnings may be, we all have to start from somewhere.

I am sure that Sister Judith knew exactly what she intended to express with her painting. And still, every viewer is allowed to see the painting with their own perceptions and interpretations. The Samenkorn taught me that many great human achievements begin as small, seemingly insignificant acts.

Warwick

Life is a continuous journey. My journey took me from Slovakia to Austria, and soon after to many other countries.

During my childhood, I didn't know much about people from different cultures. The Iron Curtain which divided Europe made us prisoners in our own country. Due to limited movement, most of our holidays and travels took place on home soil. Business trips abroad were mainly to the countries of the Eastern Bloc, like the German Democratic Republic (East Germany), Hungary, Poland, and the Soviet Union.

The fact that I didn't know about people from abroad doesn't mean there were no foreigners living in or visiting the country. There were various reasons why Slovaks and Czechs didn't know much about the Vietnamese or Africans who studied and worked in Czechoslovakia. Countries with communist governments had strong ties with Czechoslovak Socialist Republic (CSSR), and their citizens were therefore able to enter the country for a longer period. Although I asked about the foreigners I saw every now and then, my family and friends didn't tell me much. I got the impression that they weren't interested in socialising or learning more about them. In general, the Vietnamese lived their culture and customs privately, and were quite isolated from us Slovaks. However, the Vietnamese tended to be noticed by Slovaks when they had something to offer – especially when they had merchandise one couldn't buy in Czechoslovakia.

For many years, I had limited access to very scant information about other cultures, religions, values, and lifestyles. I lived protected and isolated by my family, as my parents not only liked the environment that they were used to, but were also too busy working, securing regular income from their jobs as well as tending to our garden. They generally didn't socialise much. Nevertheless, my parents greeted and treated everyone with respect. They helped others wherever they could – but they simply preferred the privacy of the flat.

While our weekend activities were spent in the garden in the village of Chorvátsky Grob, during the working week we lived in Bratislava. The flat was situated in a residential area, filled with white-grayish, multi-storey buildings that all looked the same. Although the distance between Bratislava and the Austrian capital, Vienna, amounts to only 60 km, because of communism we didn't know much about this modern, lively city's culture. We learned about the historical period of the Austro-Hungarian Empire, but only had limited information on the later democratic Austria. Censorship made it difficult to distinguish the truth from misleading information. Given that the neighbouring countries were hidden behind a wall and barbed wire, we were not able to see what lay behind. And we were too afraid to flee. Those who managed to escape began a new life in a democratic European country, America, or Canada. However, the price they had to pay for leaving the country was high, as they were often unable to see their families for many years. Moreover, the families and friends of those who fled the country were humiliated and mistreated by the authorities. Some who attempted to escape lost their lives. Others who were caught while fleeing were imprisoned. The cruelty of the regime had many different faces.

Once the borders opened after the Velvet Revolution in 1989, we started to travel more. The first time I went for a trip to Austria, I managed to cut a small part of the partly demolished barbed wire, which secured the country border. My intention was to keep it forever, as a memento of the times we survived. However, with the passing of time, I threw everything from the past away. My pioneer blouse, scarf, various badges, even the wire disappeared – I simply don't know where I stored it. After the Velvet Revolution, we realised how different the tastes, feelings, and colours of freedom are. We travelled to Monaco, Spain, Greece, and Croatia with our parents. I later travelled as a backpacker to many European countries – sometimes for a week or two, other times for a long weekend. People, cultures, religions, customs, history, architecture, music, nature, food – I finally understood how amazingly diverse the world is.

One of my most multicultural experiences, was during my studies at the University of Warwick. As an exchange student participating in the Erasmus programme, I spent six months at this well-known British university, surrounded by people from all over the world. Situated in Warwickshire, in the proximity of the River Avon, the town of Warwick has around thirty thousand inhabitants. The university campus is separated from the town of Warwick, and has an excellent infrastructure. I called it the city of students. Warwick is an amazing melting pot of people, from all corners of the world. On the very first day in the dormitory kitchen, I met students from Nigeria, Puerto Rico, Greece, China, Pakistan, India, and of course, the United Kingdom. My three friends were amazing. One introduced me to the spiciness of Indian food, and to the colourful and tolerant beliefs of Hinduism. The other charmed me with Nigerian music, and I felt motivated watching her discipline, Bible studies, and work ethic. The third beauty, from Shanghai, had a genuine interest in history, and spoke for hours about China's relations with other countries.

All of this was really surprising to me. I knew I would meet interesting people. However, the sheer number of people from different backgrounds and cultures was incredible, and my experience was far richer for it. I befriended Egyptian, French, and Malian students. The Egyptian girl soon lent me her Qur'an, after realising my interest in religion. However, it didn't take me long to realise that meeting new people wasn't always easy. The country I was born in caused many confusions and misunderstandings. The expressions on the faces of my fellow students often indicated: 'I have no idea where Slovakia is', and some actually did ask where Slovakia was. As you might imagine, I was in disbelief at this. After telling me they didn't know about Slovakia, I tried explaining that I was born in a country under a communist regime, in former Czechoslovakia. 'Ah, Czechoslovakia! Why didn't you say that earlier!' some reacted. Well, maybe because that country no longer existed? Slovak Republic was established on January 1st, 1993.

After becoming fed up with explaining, I decided to only communicate that I studied at the Vienna Business University. Other students automatically assumed that I was from Austria, and reacted accordingly. 'I love Vienna!' 'How elegant!' 'Mozart!' 'I went to ski in Austria' – people certainly knew about Austria. However, this proved to be a mistake on my part. I started to excuse people for mispronouncing my name, and for not knowing anything about my country. For some time, I accepted their ignorance. It was easier to not challenge people's thinking – but inwardly I knew that living like this wouldn't contribute to anyone's growth. I realised that if I wanted change, I would have to become the change. Therefore I started to make a real effort explaining that I am Slovak, and that Slovakia is a country in Europe, with beautiful mountains, interesting traditions, and many friendly people.

Behind Closed Doors

When I was younger, I had no idea how dangerous control can be. Unhealthy behavioural patterns aren't always obvious. Subtle isolation, for example, often flies under the radar – until it's too late. Specifically, "controllers" begin with seemingly nice gestures, leading to a situation where the victims think they should be grateful after all they've received. It's difficult to escape from somebody who is good at creating emotional dependency. Likewise, it's easier to control somebody when they feel weak.

Physical or emotional isolation serves as an insidiously powerful way to strip someone of their strength. When victims are controlled and ashamed to ask other people for help, they are more likely to do what the controlling person wants. Controlling people can be family members, clerics, teachers, or supervisors – people in a position of power. They don't have it written on their forehead, but that's the whole point. Controlling doesn't have to involve physical aggression, or threats, or even open criticism. It's often more subtle than this. Bullies belittle, and have many tools to dominate. Often, they are so good at controlling, that their victims really believe all that is said about them, and begin to think they deserve it.

When I was studying at Vienna, I was the victim of this. The controller was one of my professors. Nobody knew what was going on behind those closed doors – only he and his female students. He called it 'harmless complimenting'. In his opinion, all female students he turned his attention to should have felt unique, as they were his 'special friends'. It was a traumatic experience to enter the same office repeatedly, over many months – an office where I faced the vulgar innuendos and salacious smirks of a perverted mind.

Normally, it would start with him saying, 'Let's discuss the work so far.' I looked at him, waiting to hear feedback about the pages I wrote. Instead, I saw him simulating oral sex with his mouth and tongue. I shivered, unable to say anything. He laughed out loud, and said that I was a prude, who didn't understand humour. He expressed surprise when I refused to sleep with him, and said that nobody would ever love me, because I didn't know how to relax.

There was no way out. 'This is my life now,' I said to myself. The studies needed to be completed, and I had to endure the behaviour of a controlling and abusive person. Sometimes, I felt like dying. But whenever I sank that low, I remembered the promise I'd given to God, after surviving my suicide attempt as a teenager. I wanted to live, and I wanted the world to know what happened to me. I became sad and bitter, and all I could think of was the other female students. I knew I had to fight. After many sleepless nights and countless panic attacks, I finally found the courage to take steps against this professor. David against Goliath; I disclosed the messages he sent to me. As a result, he is no longer allowed to teach at the university.

Today, if somebody asked me how to deal with controllers, bullies, and abusers, then I would encourage them to ask for help, and encourage them not to suffer in silence. The best way to deal with controlling people is to not allow them to force their reality on anyone. They want people to fit their reality, because they don't want to face the fact that their behaviour may be wrong. After feeling so alone for so long, I finally began to enjoy life and my uniqueness again. The extreme situations of the past forced me to reflect on my own behaviour, and now I am a kinder person. It was a hard lesson to learn, but I know that I am strong and can support others who find themselves in similar situations. I changed from bitter to better.

Forest of Darkness, Forest of Light

All my life I've been wandering between normality and insanity. I am fine, then I am not. Sometimes the darkness comes without warning. I will try to describe what's happening inside me, through a story about a forest.

It is a beautiful sunny day, and I enjoy my walk through a forest. The sunrays gleam through the treetops, making the entire forest glow. Birds sing, and I find delight in the music of nature. I enjoy the beautiful plants, I smile at the butterflies chasing each other. As I walk through the forest, I feel refreshed and full of energy.

I do not know when the exact moment of transition occurs, but suddenly the whole forest turns black and grey. A strong wind begins to blow, and the sounds of nature are replaced by what seems like wailing. Covering my ears with my hands to avoid the horrible sounds, I look in all possible directions. I feel disorientated. The trees are grey, and the mysterious darkness behind them scares me. I have no idea which way to go to reach the harmonious forest again, so I try to run in any random direction. But I feel my body gradually become heavier and heavier. My body hurts so much that I am unable to walk properly, or even move. I can´t catch my breath, and despite feeling cold, I am sitting down. I assume the foetal position, still covering my ears with my hands. I can´t take these horrible sounds anymore. I close my eyes and pray this stress ends.

I wonder why I feel so bad sometimes. I am aware of my family disposition towards emotional imbalances. What affects me the most are the emotions and desires that dominate my life. My desire for love has brought me hope that one day too I will meet people who want to genuinely connect with me. But at the same time, fear, anger, and self-pity have had a hold over me for years, consuming me from the inside out. Anger meant that I didn't forgive others, nor myself. Fear took many forms. From the fear of disappointing my parents to the fear that I'd fail, fear that I'd get hurt, fear that I wouldn't finish my studies, fear that I'd fail at work, fear of what the future would bring. I pitied myself for the bad things that have happened to me in my life, asking again and again, 'Why me?' Complaining about my life hasn't always triggered sympathy – people who drain others emotionally tend to lose friends quickly.

Today, I am gradually finding solutions to my problems. As this here is my story, I am sharing what helped me. Since everyone's personal journey is different, it's not my intention to say how things should be done. I knew that after I identified my fear, desire for love, anger, and self-pity, I needed to prepare myself and take action to feel better. I've found that anger is a destructive emotion related to my past, and that I was using it to defend myself where I feared somebody or something. Today, I always try to ask myself why I'm feeling a certain way. It's better to identify the core emotion and deal with it, rather than covering it up with anger.

What was, has been, and cannot be changed. I've been hurt by people, I've hurt people. I'm sure that many of those who hurt me won't even remember it. I could go on analysing past wrongdoing, but anger won't help me move on. I chose to forgive others and myself. Fear seemed to be my primary emotion, long before anger, and therefore I needed to learn to exchange it for a healthy curiosity. Assessing new situations and choices, seeing advantages and disadvantages, helps me to not react in a fearful way. Creating a more realistic perception of life situations is important to me. I exercise my mind every day to avoid having negative emotions take over. Like fear, self-pity can become another strong paralyser. I eventually asked myself, am I so miserable and beaten that I cannot live my life to the fullest? I want to enjoy life, not waste it wallowing in self-pity. Today, I focus on my positive experiences and adventures. Living a life filled with gratitude for what I have, doesn't really leave much time for self-pity.

Love is an innate desire of every human being. With this in mind, it has not always been clear to me that love is something important to my happiness. Ultimately, we're all in the same boat – we all want to love, to be loved in return. Love has many forms, and I consider it a beautiful challenge. Helping homeless and marginalised people, expressing love – these things don't only benefit those I help, but also me. It's hard to feel self-pity or anger when people smile at you, after you gave them food or called them by their name – a name you remembered because you care.

Today, I know myself better. Still, I cannot claim that I am always in that sunny forest. What has changed, compared to the past, is that I am better equipped when the forest gets darker, and take action before it captures me.

Depression Isn't Attractive

When something terrible happens, people are generally sad about it, but that doesn't mean they are depressed. Sadness is a normal emotion. Depression is something else. Unlike temporary sadness, depression doesn't fade with time. And it can even strike without triggers.

Depression. Some of us are afraid to say this word. Mental problems are something to avoid, mental problems are something that happen 'to other people, never to me'. Sometimes, we even avoid contact with people who are depressed, because we don't know how to react. People suffering from depression are difficult to understand. It's very stressful for a sufferer to say, 'I was diagnosed with depression', because today´s society looks at diseases of the body differently than struggles of the mind. Physical illnesses are generally more accepted, people feel inclined to say, 'I am so sorry you are unwell.' But when it comes to mental disorders, people tend to look at the sufferer with a hidden suspicion: 'Are they fabricating something?' or 'Why can't they just get over whatever it is?' No wonder many people living with depression try to hide it. The open criticism can be cruel. I once told a friend that I was depressed, and she reacted by saying, 'You and depression? I thought you were stronger.' These are the exact reactions people suffering from depression are worried about, and they therefore remain silent. In a society where everyone is expected to be perfect and perform, emotional problems need to be hidden. And yet, it should be understandable that just as the body can suffer, so too can the mind.

Today we know much more about depression than we used to, and there are books, therapies, courses, and self-help groups available. Depression is not a new condition, it has been there since the earliest days of human history. Indeed, reading the Bible, I often noticed how depressed Job or David were. Today, I am sharing my own story. To me, depression is like an unwelcome creature, not only appearing without being invited, but also as a beast, trying to seize my body and mind with all its force. Depression saps your energy, it doesn't permit any rest until it manifests itself in all its cruelty.

Years back, in the midst of severe emotional pain, I wrote:

I stare at the ceiling
Time stands still
My heart jumping out of my chest
Help!
Nobody hears me
I'm trapped
Darkness everywhere
I can't breathe
Everything is hopeless

Help doesn't arrive
I lie here
It's so cold
And I'm shaking

Have you done this to me?
Or have I?
I'm trying to get some air
I can't move
My mouth wide open
My chest, so unbearably painful
My limbs so numb

What time is it?
I'm trying to get up
Without success
My bed rotates
The entire room rotates
I grab the headboard of my bed
I'm so scared
On this carousel of my loneliness

Every sufferer experiences depression differently. However, what many sufferers seem to have in common, is that depression has an impact on more than one part of their life. Life situations are less fun and interesting, and become rather overwhelming. I was easily angered, I gave up quickly. My hair was greasy, my teeth were yellow, and I would sweat often. In my mind, people were noticing these things, pointing their finger at me, while I continued to despair over my own problems and the problems of my family. Depression might be a mental illness, but it manifests in physical ways. I ate little, and had many late nights, analysing and worrying. Since I felt exhausted most of the time, even brushing my teeth was a challenge. Getting out of bed, talking to friends, going to work – everything felt like a struggle. I could no longer focus, so I simply stopped trying, and stayed in bed. I had days where I felt everything, every emotion, and it made me want to kick and scream, and then I had days when I felt almost nothing.

For me, the most exhausting part was the endless self-talks. 'I just woke up, why do I feel so tired?' 'How do I take a shower?' I tried to get up, but the darkness was unrelenting, and my body felt too weak and uncoordinated. At times I didn't sleep properly for six or seven nights in a row. Sometimes I woke in the middle of the night, sweaty and extremely thirsty. 'Why me? Why do I have to go through this? What did I do wrong? What is the time now?' I wasn't participating in life – I was merely existing, a shadow of my former self. And in the middle of that, there were moments of awareness. Awareness that life should be more than this, that this was not the way things were meant to be; yet I was helpless to change it.

What a healthy person sees as an interesting opportunity, a suffering person considers a life or death decision. It is common to overanalyse when left alone with your thoughts, and even more so when you are suffering from depression. I was afraid to take certain steps, so I procrastinated instead, and my thought patterns became more and more absurd. Overthinking can lead to serious problems; I temporarily lost the ability to see things in a positive way. I found a negative meaning behind every positive statement, questioning not only the statement, but the speaker's intention. The dark forest had closed in around me. I could not find the light.

I have been in a good place for many years now, but feeling better didn't happen overnight; it was rather a slow process. I established short-term goals relating to personal hygiene and cleaning, and built from there. Today, I'm still constantly on the alert for signs of depression recurrence, so that I can seek treatment as early as possible.

When Love Hurts

When I visited my sister in hospital for the first time, I didn't know how to react. Looking at her staring apathetically at the wall, I thought of suffering, and what that term truly means. My sister was fragile, curled up in the foetal position, lying motionless. Beaten by life. Not saying anything. Not able to sleep. I saw a woman who should have been enjoying life to the fullest, not fighting with her own body and mind. I didn't know how to speak without crying.

Memories from my past started to fill my head. I felt anxious remembering the time I spent in hospital. After so many years apart, living our own lives, I was wondering how fragile we both were. I truly believe that what we experienced during childhood had a considerable impact on us. Not only did we observe how our parents treated one another, but we clearly perceived their behaviour towards us. Frequent criticism and punishments, combined with a lack of affection and lack of physical closeness … this all stayed engraved in our souls, leaving us mistakenly believing that we somehow deserved it.

I stood in the corner of the room while my parents tried to speak with my sister. Listening to them, I was thinking about my sister's life. Up until that point, she'd lived the life of a teen-rebel – partying and dancing until the late hours. All of that changed, however, when a man offered her a lift home from a disco one night. For a long time, I didn't know anything about this, as it had happened in Switzerland, and my sister was too traumatised and scared to share her pain with anyone. Years went by, and she fell in love with a man much older than her. They married and lived in a strange love triangle for years. Was there another woman? No, only his mother, who loved her son and kept controlling his wife, because in her opinion my sister was far too young, too inexperienced, and poor. Therefore, she "needed" to be told what to do. My sister lived far away, and I didn't know of her suffering. One day she called me and cried. When she complained, I thought it was normal. After all, married couples often go through difficult times. Then, suddenly, she stopped contacting me. I called her several times, but she didn't pick up. I tried again and again.

Then I heard her breathing:

'Hello, are you there?' I asked.

Apart from breathing, I heard nothing.

'Please, say something,' I begged.

My sister's reaction was truly unexpected. 'Hi, I wasn't sure it was you, I thought somebody tried to imitate your voice. You know that the world today is full of spies and telephone tapping. I need to hang up.'

I sat there, thinking about the words I just heard. Confused, worried – nothing made sense.

A long time ago, my father and I sat down together to talk about our past mistakes. My father understood that his ways were too strict, and decided to offer a helping hand. But standing in the room, looking at my sister lying on the bed, dressed in clothes provided by the hospital, I felt like there was no hope. I kept asking myself, 'How can somebody survive so much suffering?' When I finally found the courage to speak to her, there was no response. She kept staring into the emptiness, trying to escape reality. Life was too much to bear. All I really wanted to say was, 'I love you, my dear sister. Please get up.'

Needless to say, the whole experience was painful. I learnt a lot from visiting my sister in the hospital, as there were some behaviours to consider, behaviours that I was less aware of when I was there myself. Hospitals can be intimidating, and visiting a loved one there is a difficult and scary process. However, as soon as my sister felt better and started to speak, she didn't want pity. She wanted to be taken seriously – she longed for empathy and at times closeness. The most important thing for me was to realise that my sister needed compassion, love, support, humour, and genuine non-judgemental interest in what she was going through.

Today, my sister is in a new loving relationship. She feels more accepted for the person she is. Love doesn't hurt anymore.

London

I'm standing in front of a crowd of people, holding a microphone in my sweaty hands. I'm looking out into the sea of faces and wondering why all the traditional tips for dealing with stage fright – imagine everyone naked, breathe and count to ten – aren't working.

I am vulnerable. I do not want to be judged.

The first time I shared my mental health journey with an audience of fifty people, I was so nervous, but I tried not to show it. I reminded myself of my mission – the reason why I started to speak about mental health in the first place. I told myself, "Eva, you care. You care about all the people who suffer in silence – people like you. Be the voice of the voiceless, be the one who speaks about hope. Now is the moment to be brave."

Bravery has many faces. It's the person who speaks up when everyone else watches injustice. It's the person who fights the good fight, until the very end. And sometimes, it's the person who accepts their defeat, and finds the strength to move on. My own courage came from a place of personal experience. I had suffered, I was suffering, so I made the choice to act. But still, that did not mean I was fearless.

Courageous people are not without fear. They only learn to embrace discomfort, and act despite their fear. Fear exists, and we will never be completely free from it. Fear is not always bad. It keeps us safe, and stops us from acting recklessly. But sometimes, it also keeps us from achieving success. It's better to acknowledge fear, rather than deny its existence. If we deny fear, it only goes deeper, forming a barrier to the life that we are meant to live.

I wanted to limit fear's power. So, I started really listening to what my fear was saying. This might seem like an unusual approach, but by actually learning to appreciate my own fear and where it came from, I was able to dismiss it, and stop myself believing the stories it was telling me. I also started connecting to my body more – jogging, doing yoga to relax and ease my tension. I reached out, asking for help, and for meaningful communication. I wanted to be able to laugh and cry, to be part of a community with others. And by giving myself this opportunity, I learnt that I don't have to do it all alone. I believe in trusting others – that when you trust someone you create chances and opportunities not just for you, but for them too. We often underestimate the power that connection and community can have on the human spirit.

Fear chooses mediocrity. Courage chooses the extraordinary. Sometimes, when people live for so long in their perception of their own inadequacy, they become unable to see their beauty. They simply stop believing in their potential for greatness. Imagine learning to be courageous. I believe that by starting small, and then repeatedly practising, one can learn certain behaviours. Standing in front of an audience for the first time, I felt nauseous. I thought that everyone would be able to see my shaky hands, that they would judge me for it. It was only through repeated experience of standing on stage in front of audiences, that I was able to decrease these negative emotions. With the passing of time, I became more comfortable with being uncomfortable. I still feel fear whenever I step on stage, but I'm brave enough to speak anyway.

Changing my focus was key to this. Today, I focus less on myself. I worry less about what could happen, such as losing my voice mid-sentence, and instead focus on my mission. I focus on the positive impact that talking about mental health can have, and in doing so I feel less stressed about public speaking. I have learnt to be more rational in assessing the possible outcomes of situations. When you lack confidence, you tend to catastrophise – you see only the negative consequences of actions. It's very important to think through opportunities, to assess their value.

Today, I believe in my ability to succeed.

Years ago, fearful and with little confidence, I would never have spoken in front of an audience. Now, looking back, I can only imagine the cost of letting these fears rule me, of letting them sap my confidence. I think about all of the adventures I would have missed, and the beauty left undiscovered. If you don't embrace opportunities, you can only guess at what might have been, at the cost of a life not lived.

After I moved to London, I didn't just speak at events. I co-organised conferences, enabling other people to speak about the things that matter to them. I noticed that the more I dared, and the more I was out there in front of other people, the more doors opened, and the more talents I discovered. It wasn't luck that brought me here, but courage and dedication.

Next time, when you face a situation such as public speaking, don't ask yourself about the worst thing that could happen. Instead, focus on the best thing that could happen.

I think that we are meant to be brave. Being brave means living an authentic life, to persevere, and to love. Because bravery is an act of love.

Courageous people are game changers. Courageous people can make this world a better place. That's why we need to start. Not just we, you. When you go first, other people will be inspired to discover their own courage.

Forgiveness and Violets

Forgiveness and Violets

"Forgiveness is the fragrance that the violet sheds on the heel that has crushed it." Mark Twain

When you picked up this book, there's a good chance that you might have been wondering about the title. The poetic words above – my favourite Mark Twain quote – convey forgiveness as leaving a pleasant scent after the pain caused.

In my life, I have often struggled to forgive. After people mistreated me, I felt anger, and I held onto this anger. In some way, it felt like the anger was mine, as if it belonged to me – nobody could take it away. There was a voice in my head, constantly reminding me of the reasons why I had the right to feel negative emotions. For years I had been neglected emotionally, and punished physically, for things I didn't see as terrible enough to be beaten for. I became somebody whose thinking and acting was based on shame and guilt. Shame told me who I was, and guilt told me that everything I did was bad or not good enough.

Today, I am aware of the fact that my experiences contributed to this negative thinking. There were situations where I couldn't cope with heavy pressure from my parents, and later from others whom I depended on. I acknowledge that I had to go through what I went through, to get to where I am today. I choose to be an observer, rather than somebody who needs to judge other people.

Sometimes, people who have never experienced love and physical affection on a daily basis don't comprehend it. It's like an unreachable dream. On my part, I was full of extremes – longing for human warmth on one side and isolating myself on the other. Being in so much emotional pain was exhausting. It started to eat me from the inside out. In my heart, I knew that I didn't want to feel miserable any more. I didn't want to give those who had hurt me any more power over my life. I felt that forgiveness and acceptance in my situation would be a longer process, but I started to have compassion for myself, and gave myself time to search for answers and heal.

Forgiveness doesn't mean condoning unkindness, or forgetting what has happened. I didn't forget the pain, and I probably never will. Forgiving is something I did for myself, because I didn't want to be a victim, filled with fear and anger. Although I would have liked discussions, I couldn't expect those who hurt me to fully see what they did. The greatest quality of forgiveness, is that the person forgiving doesn't need anything from those who caused them pain. It is ultimately your decision to let go, or to hold on to your pain and anger. Forgiveness is courageous. By combining this with other powerful resources, like love and prayer, I have ensured that I don't go to sleep angry. I have ensured that I no longer spend the day with my own negative thoughts. I forgive myself and others. That's more courageous than anything else I have ever been capable of doing.

Walk With Me

During my walks by the River Thames, I see many violets. Their beauty strengthens my creative ambitions, and I am inspired by their uniqueness and quiet dignity. When I look into the glittery water, watching the birds and surrounding greenery, I am filled with joy. I love nature, because I feel so close to the Source. For those unfamiliar with this term, I am referring to God – the Source of creation. Life in London is filled with noise and distractions, and spending time in silence helps me to relax and think about connections. As a society, we focus too much on goal setting and achieving, and the end result is a feeling of disconnection. We are disconnected from our true calling, and from each other. Only when we stop comparing ourselves to others, can we truly realise that all, ultimately, is one. Where society divides, nature unifies.

The time I spend in silence at the river helps me to understand one of the most important lessons that I have learnt – life is joy. A given set of rules and beliefs can restrict a person's view, and this was certainly true for me. I was taught to set targets, and focus on achieving them. To a certain extent, my upbringing prevented me from experiencing what life could offer. Today, I am open to new ways of seeing and doing things. I have become a passionate cook, traveller, and explorer of different cultures. All of these things, and more, enrich my life and my being, in ways that I could previously never have imagined.

Walk with me for a bit, and I will share some of my stories. I'm a writer who tries to inform and inspire. Most of the insights from this book, I gained from what I experienced myself. I have been a writer for many years. Since my early teens, I have written stories, poems, and travel journals. Sometimes, I have moments when I don't feel inspiration. Doubting is part of who I am – a human hoping to find a deeper meaning in things. I can't change what happened in the past, but I choose how I look at my life now. Choosing to feel better, and having the strength to do this, is a powerful thing, and I have taken many steps to be at peace with myself.

Some people die wondering how exciting life could have been. I choose to be different. I want to do the small things in the best way, without demanding (from God) big opportunities. I don't want to wait forever for big things to happen. So, I grasp my opportunities. As of today, I have been salsa dancing for over ten years – this has helped me to discover a very personal and unique way of expression. Now, it is time for you to find your own. Choose to walk away from negativity, and inspire others, helping them to find their own courage, and begin their own journey towards happiness.

Through my experiences, I have found my own calling, my own sense of purpose. I chose love and enthusiasm for life, and I allowed myself to feel joyful, and experience the best that life can offer. I let myself be happy, and to feel the positivity that only emotions like love can bring. When you find these yourself, you will know. Believe me, they are contagious!

Thank you

Writing stories about my life was a surreal process. None of this would have been possible without the help of my friends, who have contributed to my healing and growth, and helped me to share my writing voice with the world.

A very special thanks to Will and Sue Ballantyne for building a community of people, in London, who helped and continue helping each other with information related to mental health. For years you supported me on my journey of discovery. The courses I attended and volunteered at enabled me to connect with other people, in a very open, non-judgemental way.

I also want to thank Irene Berra and Alessandro Iacovangelo for sharing their thoughts and opinions with me after reading early drafts of some of my stories. I appreciate your patience, invaluable comments, and great sense of humour.

Thanks to everyone on the publishing team. It is because of your efforts and encouragement that I finished my book. Sometimes when I was tired I looked at the beautiful book cover you had cleverly designed for me, and it gave me motivation. Special thanks to Richard McMunn for your specialist insight and ongoing support in bringing my stories to life, and to Jordan Cooke, my editor – I will always treasure our thought exchange during the editing of my book. Thank you for your work and dedication.

Finally, thank you to the friendly employees of the Wandsworth Town and Battersea Libraries. I spent months working on my stories while enjoying your company and reactions to my many questions. I am forever grateful for your respectful treatment.